Great Railway Journeys in
Asia

David Bowden

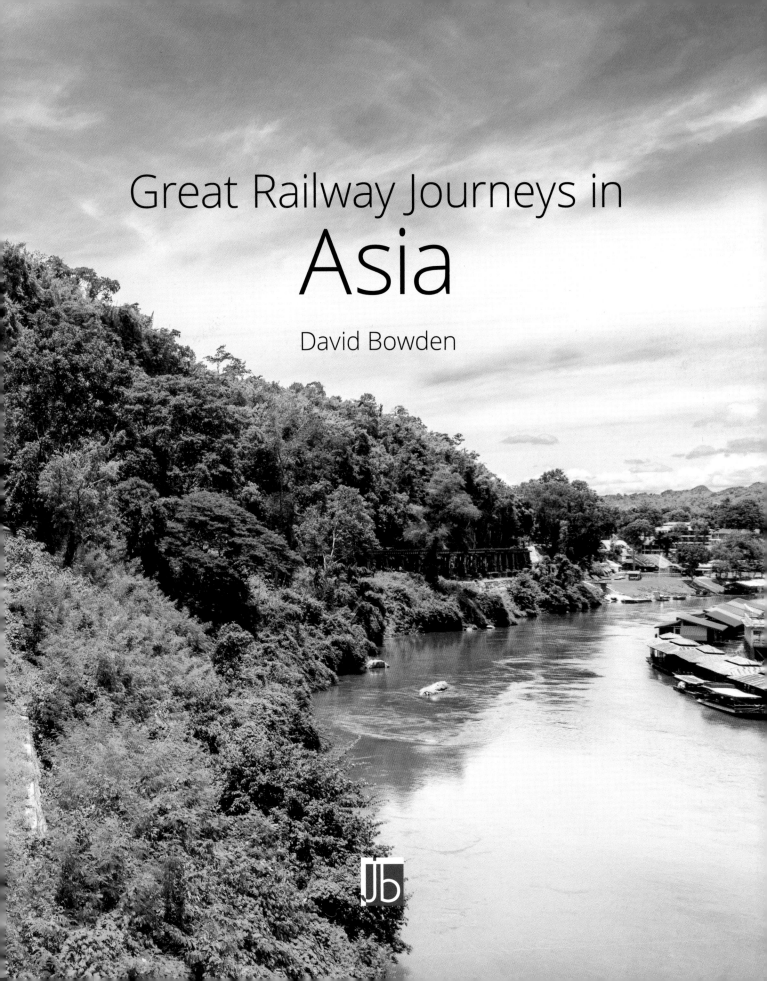

Great Railway Journeys in
Asia

David Bowden

CONTENTS

page 1 *Seven Stars in Kyushu* at cherry blossom time.

pages 2–3 The train from Bangkok to Nam Tock travelling over the Wampo Viaduct.

Opposite Tourist steam trains occasionally journey along Sri Lanka's rail network.

INTRODUCTION

With the numerous transportation modes available to travellers, few parts of the world remain unexplored. Developments in the second half of the nineteenth century enabled more people to travel, initially on rail, then on other forms of transportation.

Inventors had been dabbling with steam as a means of movement and transportation, with British inventor Richard Trevithick attributed with building the first steam locomotive in 1802. The era of mass transport began unwittingly in 1825, when the steam locomotive developed by George Stephenson (named Locomotion No. 1) hauled passengers on England's Stockton to Darlington Public Railway. Within five years the first commercial railway opened between Manchester and Liverpool. These developments were so well received that within 20 years of Stephenson's locomotive plying the tracks, Britain, closely followed by continental Europe,

had thousands of kilometres of track. For the first time, the masses could travel cheaply over long distances. The concept soon went global as European entrepreneurs began exploring and exploiting other parts of the world. Trains were proposed for Asia, too, with the first beginning operations in Madras (Mumbai) in 1853.

Asia is considered as the land mass bordered by Europe to the west, the Pacific Ocean to the east, the Arctic Ocean to the north and the Indian Ocean to the south. For the purposes of this book, Asia is compartmentalized as South Asia, Southeast Asia and North Asia. Asia also includes the world's two largest countries – China and parts of Russia – so is well served by rail networks. This makes it one of the most exciting parts of the world for train exploration.

While Asia forges ahead, with buildings rising ever more skyward and railways extending into uncharted territory, the

golden era of steam-rail travel lives on in some parts and still lures travellers to Asia. Although most Asian cities have modern downtowns similar to those in other parts of the world, all have cultural and historical elements that make them unique and entice inquisitive travellers.

Travel involves the journey and destinations along the way as much as the arrival, so each chapter in this book has information on leading tourist sights and attractions at the point of departure, on route and at the point of arrival, so that travellers can better plan their journeys. Information is given on what makes each destination and journey unique, and there is a brief description of the railway's history. Grand hotels, historic sites, iconic bars and famous restaurants are also mentioned, along with railway services and facilities. Some grand hotels, for example, became as important as the destinations, with comments like 'when in Singapore stay in the Raffles' being a common refrain from those fortunate enough to travel in the mid to late nineteenth centuries.

Many people travel to relive what was a golden era of travel

and to experience several luxurious trains that recreate a period of refined elegance. However, they do this at a price, because such iconic trains charge a hefty tariff. Mere mortals use public railways, and while the experience may not be as grand, these railways serve the purpose of transporting travellers from one place to the next.

Those singular trains that have names such as *Seven Stars in Kyushu* or the *Eastern & Oriental Express* are written in italics throughout the text. Trains that operate merely as a service on a railway line have been written in normal font. For example, while many may consider that a train journey such as the Trans-Siberian Railway consists of an actual train, there is in fact no such train but rather many trains that operate on the line across Siberia.

Opposite The train to Lhasa in Tibet passes over the Tanggula Pass at 5,068 m (16,627 ft), making it the world's highest rail route.

Below The narrow gauge Darjeeling Himalayan Railway is one of the world's most acclaimed railway journeys.

EXPANDING NEW HORIZONS

While some consider the best days of rail travel to have passed, many point to the expansion of world railways. Celebrated author and train traveller Paul Theroux noted in his book about travel on Chinese trains during the 1980s, *Riding the Iron Rooster*, that the Chinese could build cities faster than they could print them on maps and build railways quicker than they could show them with black lines.

Fast forward a few decades and the expansion of Chinese railways continues to power on, as previously inaccessible parts of the country are rapidly brought into the network. This is not only occurring in China. Advances are also being made into neighbouring countries under what is known as China's Belt and Road Initiative, which is rapidly changing Asia's rail landscape.

This initiative, involving massive global infrastructure development, was first adopted by the Chinese government in 2013. The plan is to involve 70 countries through direct investment or joint ventures. This new 'Silk Road' initiative involves overland rail and road links principally throughout Asia, but also in other parts of the world. Maritime routes are a key element, with the Chinese sphere of influence now accounting for 65 per cent of the world's population and 40 per cent of global GDP.

While not without its critics, the initiative is certainly opening up new rail frontiers and facilitating the export of Chinese goods. Passengers also benefit because several countries, especially China, have opened or will soon open new destinations with the introduction of high-speed rail. Despite the concerns expressed in some quarters regarding debt burden to developing countries, the news appears to be good for rail travellers.

An exciting prospect for train aficionados is the possibility of travelling by rail from Singapore to Europe, with the only sections currently without connectivity being those from Aranyaprathet (south-east Thailand) to Poipet (north-west Cambodia), and the Cambodian capital Phnom Penh through to Ho Chi Minh City in southern Vietnam. For some reason, this latter stretch of 228 km (142 miles) was never connected by rail, but that could change with China's Belt and Road Initiative. Meanwhile, dedicated train travellers can contemplate the possibility of one day using continuous rail from Singapore through Asia and across the vastness of Russia on the Trans-Siberian Railway. From here, there are lines to other European destinations, including its extremities – Karskaya in north-west Russia (north), Pozzallo, Sicily (south) and Tralee, Ireland (west). The recent opening of the railway through Lao PDR (Laos) has now made continuous rail journeying from

Above The route to Tenom is currently the only railway line on Borneo, the third largest island in the world.

Opposite Trains like India's *Palace on Wheels* offer the opportunity to travel in and experience nostalgic luxury.

Asia to Europe possible, be it a different route that extends from north-east Thailand (Nong Khai), over the Mekong River through Vientiane, the Lao capital, northwards through Lao PDR to Boten on the Chinese border and then all the way to Kunming on the Chinese rail network. This section of rail completes a continuous line that commences in Singapore, through Malaysia, Thailand, China and a dozen countries as far as Lagos in Portugal. This exciting new route covers some 19,000 km (11,806 miles) and would take several weeks of continuous travel.

BEYOND THE ORDINARY

Choosing the great railway journeys anywhere is subjective, as different travellers have different expectations and requirements. Travellers also measure 'greatness' on different scales, but an attempt has been made here to include iconic journeys in countries considered safe to travel in and relatively easy to access. In addition, some lesser known journeys in more remote parts have been included for more adventurous travellers to consider.

Journeys have been selected in an attempt to cater to a variety of travellers – from one of the longest journeys (Trans-Siberian) to one of the shortest (Penang Funicular); from one of the best value for money (Tenom) to one of the most luxurious (E&O); from steam (*North Borneo Railway*) to the world's most advanced (Japanese Bullet); from one of the slowest (Tadami Line) to the fastest (Maglev); from below sea level across China's Taklamakan Desert to one of the highest regions in the world (Tibet). Some journeys involve steam locomotives, magnetic levitation (Maglev) or rack-and-pinion rail, embracing the ultimate in luxury to the most rudimentary levels of comfort. Some journeys are made in the sweltering heat and humidity of Southeast Asia, some across the parched deserts of Western China and others in the freezing winter of the Russian steppes.

The world of rail travel is rapidly changing and advancing, and this brings with it alterations in schedules, frequency and infrastructure, so use this book as a guide. However, it is essential to fully research any journey before heading off on an Asian rail adventure. Having an open mind and the ability to adapt to ever-changing travel conditions is important, especially on some of the more remote and less used Asian railways.

TRANS-SIBERIAN RAILWAY

AN EPIC JOURNEY

It is probably no surprise that Russia, the world's largest country, has the world's longest railway network, stretching 9,259 km (5,752 miles) from Vladivostok on the Pacific Ocean in the east, to Moscow in the west. As a point of reference, another epic train journey, Australia's *Indian Pacific* from Sydney to Perth, is a mere 4,352 km (2,704 miles) long.

Just as there is no one Silk Road but rather several routes, there is no train with the title 'Trans-Siberian Railway'. However, the various railways connecting Vladivostok with Moscow across a third of the globe have appealed to travellers for decades. The route's great length and immense scope for off-train exploration have made it a pilgrimage for global train travellers and railway enthusiasts. Alternatively, for those with limited time, the journey can be completed without optional disembarkations in as little as 143 hours or six full days. As such, it is a journey that many travellers aspire to take. Those who have completed this adventure wear the experience as a badge of honour.

Proposals for a rail connection from Moscow and European Russia to Vladivostok on the Pacific Ocean were first suggested in 1858. The Crimean War delayed further discourse until 1875, when the first plan was outlined. After much discussion, the project started in Vladivostok in 1891 with a connection made to Moscow in 1903, including a train ferry across Lake Baikal. The line around the southern section of Lake Baikal was completed in 1905. Part of the initial route crossed Manchuria and despite it being on Chinese territory, it was a shorter distance and the tracks were cheaper to install due to the flat terrain.

The journey is far more than just one train on one line. It consists of several interconnected routes that may be taken in various ways. The original Trans-Siberian route was built during Tsarist times to connect Moscow's Yaroslavl Station to the port of

Opposite Trains on the Trans-Siberian Railway pass through a variety of landscapes including the coniferous forest of Siberia.

Vladivostok. The line was opened in 1905, and contributed to the taming and settling of the Siberian wilderness. It helped consolidate Russian control of Siberia and the Pacific provinces. By the 1950s the whole journey was double tracked and it is now electrified.

All trains are well heated to ward off winter chills, and passengers can normally ride in deluxe first-class compartments (two berths and en suite) or second class (four berths/compartment). However, first-class sleeper wagons were recently removed so it is best to check when making a booking. Solo travellers or couples requiring privacy need to book all four seats in a compartment.

TRACK NOTES

Today, the core Trans-Siberian route is a fully electrified, double-track line that serves as a trunk line of the Russian Railway network. It is a heavily used freight route and a passenger lifeline for many communities along the way, as well as an ever-popular route for tourists and travellers. Many local families and business passengers use the train, with a predominance of Chinese and Russians on board.

The classic approach is to begin the journey in Moscow and travel eastwards across the Soviet Union on the daily and year-round *Rossiya* train to Vladivostok. This unbroken journey involves several on the train. Naturally, the journey can be made in reverse departing from Vladivostok, although going from west to east is more common for tourists.

Interestingly, while few railway travellers consider a round trip across Russia, railway-travel purists frown on flying to Trans-Siberian terminal cities to begin the journey, and advocate travelling overland by train from London, Paris or other European railway hubs, while also continuing the rail journey from its eastern end. Popular alternatives to the all-Russian journey are the *Trans-Mongolian Railway* (page 18) and the Trans-Manchurian Railway options, where the Siberian leg of the trip terminates in China, with Beijing being the ultimate destination for both routes. The *Trans-Mongolian Railway* veers off the main line through the steppes of Mongolia and on to Beijing in northern China.

WELCOME ABOARD

In Soviet times Vladivostok was closed to foreigners due to its strategic importance as a naval base. Instead, foreign travellers were directed to Nakhodka via a branch line operating from the main Trans-Siberian route at Ussunysk. An alternative route across eastern Siberia is via the 'Second Trans-Siberian' Railway, the once-elusive BAM line (although rarely spelt out, this stands for Baikal-Amur-Mainline), which operates to the north of the original route, deviating near Tayshet (4,522 km/2,810 miles east of Moscow), and terminating at the Pacific port of Sovetskaya Gavan.

The Trans-Siberian line was built in an effort to develop and better extract the region's resources. The railway was a lifeline, but also a conduit for the exploitation of Russia's natural wealth, in a similar manner to America's Trans-Continental railroads. In Soviet times a trip across Siberia offered a window on a society shaped by communism and largely closed to Western visitors. The mystique of the Soviet Union was what lured many visitors; it was as if Siberia was a place that Russians endured, but Westerners happily visited.

President Gorbachev's rule brought an end to the old Russian regime. With it, the Russian economy opened to foreign investment, and business entrepreneurship is now evident all over Siberia. Yet everything is not necessarily what it seems. For those willing to experience a panorama of thousands of kilometres of passing birch forests, there are numerous glimpses of the foreboding, long-forbidden and fascinating other world that is Siberian Russia.

The *Rossiya* is the Trans-Siberian route's flagship train, offering some of the best accommodation, especially for those travelling in first class (Train One travels eastwards, and Train Two westwards). This train features all sorts of novel technology previously unknown to Russian railways, such as air-conditioning and fully operational, retention toilets. For travellers looking to fill in the long line on their map between Moscow and the Pacific, this is the most comfortable option. However, since the *Rossiya* is largely reserved for through passengers, it is not necessarily available to passengers wishing to make stopovers at intermediate destinations. For those looking to alight from the train and explore, there is a variety of other trains that operate on the whole route or on different sections. These occasionally use older (or at least unrefurbished), traditional carriages. To better experience Siberia and break up the long journey, it is recommended that visitors consider at least one stopover. The principal cities along the way from west to east are Perm, Omsk, Novosibirsk, Krasnoyarsk, Irkutsk, Ulan-Ude, Chita, Khabarovsk and Vladivostok.

Opposite top The restaurant car of the *Zarengold* private train.

Opposite below Accommodation on the *Zarengold* train varies with the classic category having twin berths, toilets at the carriage end and showers shared between two carriages.

Left In addition to keeping Russian train carriages clean and passengers well stocked with snacks and water, the *provodnista* keeps passengers informed of the next stop, and helps them on and off their train.

Opposite The Trans-Siberian Railway passes Lake Baikal, which stores about 22 per cent of the world's fresh surface water – more than all the water contained in the Great Lakes in North America.

One of the characteristics of the older stock was the coal-fired samovar at the end of each carriage. Samovars were enormous, rising nearly the full height of the corridor, and were used to supply hot water for tea and, once cooled, a clean source of drinking water. The older carriages featured a chimney for exhaust that extended through the roof, so that, despite an electric locomotive leading the train, the aroma of coal smoke provided a nostalgic ambiance. Nowadays the samovar is more commonly heated by bottled gas.

One feature of Russian trains is the car attendant, usually a woman, known as a *provodnista*, who helps travellers. Two attendants are assigned to each carriage and work half-day shifts. They check in passengers on boarding the train and ensure that they are in the correct compartment and seat (there is no open/ unreserved seating on long-distance trains). In addition, they sell snacks, souvenirs and instant noodles, and remove rubbish. With withering looks, they also maintain order and behaviour on the journey, but they often respond with friendliness to a smile and *spasiba* ('thank you' in Russian).

Trains skirt Lake Baikal in the middle of the Siberian taiga and pass some impressive mountainous sights in southern Siberia. Baikal is the world's largest and deepest lake, containing about 22 per cent

of the Earth's fresh water. The average depth is 730 m (2,395 ft), with the deepest points being more than 1,609 m (5,279 ft) below the surface. It is believed that the volume of water represents 80 per cent of all the fresh water in Russia. The lake is 96 km (400 miles) long and is estimated to be 20 to 25 million years old. It has been a site of human settlement since the Stone Age, with identifiable human activity dating back to at least 15,000 years.

Lake Baikal is one of the highlights of the Trans-Siberian route, as well as on both the Trans-Manchurian and Trans-Mongolian routes. It is situated in eastern Siberia, south-east of the Siberian capital of Irkutsk in the Buryat Autonomous Republic. The lake is surrounded by mountains, which were a considerable impediment to the Trans-Siberian Railway in its early years. Difficulties in engineering around the lake delayed completion. Between 1900 and 1904, trains were ferried across the lake between Port Baikal and Mysovaya on the eastern shore. An extension around the southwestern portion of the lake was initially opened in 1904, although operational difficulties did not completely do away with train ferries until 1916. The third major change to the Lake Baikal route occurred in 1950, when the Soviets dammed the Angara River, which flooded the valley below Irkutsk and raised the level of the lake. Avoiding the dam and the lower Angara Valley required a completely new alignment built south from Irkutsk to reach a junction at Slyudyanka. This new line, among the most impressive parts of the Trans-Siberian journey, required some expensive engineering using reverse loops to maintain a steady gradient. The climb on the cut-off begins at the eastern end of the Irkursk passenger station. Near the summit of the line the gradient reaches 2.3 per cent – the steepest on the entire route. The sinuous descent towards Lake Baikal offers stunning summer and winter views. East of Slyudyanka the line hugs the southeastern shore, with the mountains to the north visible beyond the far side of the lake.

A truncated portion of the 1904 line, 89 km (53 miles) long, known as the Krugobaikalka, is retained for local services and excursions along the rugged western shore from Slyudyanka to Port Baikal. This route features numerous tunnels as it skirts the lake on a rock shelf. It is one of the scenic diversions available for travellers who take the time to explore the Baikal region. For many visitors Lake Baikal is the destination, with this immense inland sea offering outdoor tourism in warmer months and a frozen lake surface traversed by hovercraft and vehicles in winter. Ferries span the lake at various points and a hydrofoil runs the length of it, while its northern reaches are accessible via the BAM route.

ATTENTION TO DETAIL

It is important to note that the railway operates on Moscow time throughout the journey, despite crossing eight or nine time zones. The concept of time was noted by Paul Theroux in *Riding the Iron Rooster*. He wrote: 'Every day is the same on the Trans-Siberian:

that is one of its reassuring aspects.' The best time to admire the Siberian landscape is in summer (May to September), when the daylight hours are longest. Winter, in heated carriages, offers a very different charm that also appeals, as do the less crowded carriages and villages.

Tickets can be problematic because it is not possible to purchase an open ticket and hop on and off the train; it is an all-reserved, long-distance train, with every passenger allocated a sleeping berth. Tickets are allocated on specific days, and have a train, carriage and berth number. Those who want to sightsee at specific cities along the way can make stopovers by using separate tickets for each train. These can be purchased from stations or via online pre-booking before departure. With all the ticket permutations, it makes good sense for foreigners to use the services of a professional travel agency that specializes in international rail journeys.

Two routes branch off this line to provide access to China. The *Trans-Mongolia Railway* (page 18) heads to Beijing via the Mongolian capital Ulan Bator. Train enthusiasts argue that in the warmer months this is the preferred journey, because it combines two iconic train routes that pass through the contrasting landscapes of Siberia's taiga and Mongolia's Gobi Desert. In winter the Manchurian route offers amazing snow-clad landscapes and villages. Venturing forth in below-zero temperatures offers leg-stretching opportunities unlike anything experienced in warmer climes.

A Trans-Manchurian route operates through northern China from Chita to Beijing, passing through cities such as Harbin, famous for its International Ice and Snow Sculpture Festival in January, which features ice carvings illuminated by colourful lighting. Harbin is the capital of China's most northeasterly province of Heilongjiang, formerly known as Manchuria. After word, add:

Private trains such as *Zarengold* and *Golden Eagle Trans-Siberian Express* provide a more luxurious train experience, set departures and organized off-train excursions.

Left Passengers need to choose the season to travel on the Trans-Siberian Railway carefully as it varies markedly from winter to summer, with the town of Yakutsk having an average December high temperature of -35° C (-32° F).

TRANS-MONGOLIAN RAILWAY

FROM TAIGA TO DESERT

Passengers who travel eastwards all the way to Vladivostok on the Trans-Siberian Railway (which, as stated, is not a train but a route, page 10) effectively terminate their journey at a railway dead end. There are no trains beyond Vladivostok, although those planning to continue their journeys of discovery on Japanese railways could consider the 21-hour ferry crossing across the Sea of Japan from Vladivostok to Sakaiminato on the main Japanese island of Honshu.

A popular alternative to travelling all the way to Vladivostok is to detour through Mongolia along the famous *Trans-Mongolian Railway* route that traverses vast, grassy plains, or steppes, plus the Gobi Desert. The *Trans-Mongolian Railway* is one of several trains that link Beijing with Moscow

The *Trans-Mongolian Railway* is a journey 7,621 km (4,735 miles) long that shares the same track as the Trans-Siberian Railway up to Ulan-Ude, where it branches off from the main line to head southwards towards Mongolia and China.

The other route is the Trans-Manchurian Railway, which operates through Siberia along the Trans-Siberian Railway route to Chita before heading south into China and passing Harbin, the capital of Heilongjiang Province, formerly known as Manchuria.

Train enthusiasts maintain that the *Trans-Mongolian Railway* linking Moscow and Beijing is the more interesting of the rail connections between China and Russia. It passes through Russia, Siberia, Mongolia and China, and presents numerous sightseeing opportunities along the way for travellers who want to break their journey.

TRACK NOTES

Today, through Trans-Mongolian express passenger trains operate scheduled departures on a weekly basis, although there are other long-distance trains as well. East-bound trains depart from Moscow late on Tuesday evening, while west-bound trains depart Beijing every Wednesday morning.

This is a substantially newer railway line. Construction began after the Second World War. By 1950 it had opened from the junction with the Trans-Siberian line at Zaudinski near the Soviet city of Ulan-Ude, to reach southwards to the Mongolian capital at Ulan Bator (Ulaanbaatar). By 1955 the railway spanned Mongolia, running 1,111 km (690 miles) to reach the Chinese border at Erenhot (Erlian).

WELCOME ABOARD

Passengers for the weekly train through to Beijing gather on Tuesday evening at Yaroslavski Station in Central Moscow. A 'United Nations' of travellers establish themselves in their compartments on the Chinese train with Moscow-Ulan Bator-Beijing carriage signage. Reservations are obligatory and passengers can book deluxe two-berth compartments (the upper berth can be folded away in order for both passengers to sit on the lower berth), which have a shower hose that is shared with the adjoining compartment. Other passengers have to wash the best they can in the toilets or

Above The railway in Mongolia is used to transport goods and minerals over long distances through terrain such as these grassland steppes.

sinks in each car. Most compartments are four berth, with two lower and two upper bunks, and luggage storage under the lower berths, between the upper berths and above the door. First-class and second-class compartments are available – many passengers claim that they are basically the same and that the extra charge for first class is not warranted. There is a samovar that dispenses boiling water at the end of each carriage.

Visas for Mongolia and China need to be obtained before departure, as they are not available at immigrations checkpoints along the way.

The restaurant car and the culinary delights dispensed here change in each country that the train passes through (Russia, Mongolia and China). Most passengers find the meals served acceptable and inexpensive, with roubles and US dollars the only currencies accepted.

The train stops every few hours to enable passengers sufficient time to stretch their legs, and to purchase snacks and beverages from platform vendors along the way. The main cities that the train passes through on the first three days include Perm, Ekaterinburg, Omsk, Novosibirsk and Krasnoyarsk.

On day four, the train travels around Lake Baikal and passengers have good views of the world's deepest freshwater lake. By this stage new friendships have been made and there tends to be a party atmosphere on the train. Passengers wishing to explore the lake alight at Irkutsk. Beyond Irkutsk, the train travels along the foreshore of the lake for even better views.

On day five, the train reaches Ulan-Ude, scenically located between the Khama Daban and Tsaga Daban Ranges. This historic city has been on a tea-trading route and has been a trading centre for centuries. It is among potential stopover destinations for travellers on a variety of Trans-Siberian / Trans-Mongolian journeys, with attractions like the Russian Buddhist Centre and a large locomotive works. Here, trains heading to Mongolia uncouple their electric locomotives and change to diesel power – typically a Soviet-era 2M62 locomotive.

Just after Ulan-Ude the landscape becomes arid, with grassy expanses, brushy vegetation and few trees. South of Ulan-Ude, the line follows the Selange River on its journey to the Mongolia border.

Naushki is the Siberian frontier post where travellers experience a prolonged customs and immigration stop of two to three hours. Expect another extended stop on the Mongolian side of the frontier at Sukhbaator, where the Russian Railway's locomotives are replaced by similar models operated by Mongolian Railway.

Through travellers will delight in the Mongolian Railway's dining car added to the train, as it offers variety from its Russian counterpart and is claimed by many to be of higher quality.

Once on the move, free from the rigours of immigration procedures, trains cross the Eastern Mongolian steppes towards the national capital, Ulan Bator. The railway is largely a single-track line that curves and sweeps through a sublimely barren landscape that is apparent on the morning of day six. *Gers* (round, tent-like structures also called yurts), home to nomadic pastoralists, can be seen in the grassland pastures.

This is the land of the infamous Asian horse-riding military strategist and conqueror Temujin, better known by his assumed name Genghis Khan. His empire once spanned the continent centred at Karakorum, an ancient city south-west of Ulan Bator.

Later in the morning of day six, the train stops for some 30 minutes in the capital before heading for the Gobi Desert. Ulan Bator is Mongolia's largest city, and although characterized by uninspiring architecture it makes for a fascinating sojourn, as well

as a jumping-off point for explorations in Mongolia. The city is famously cold in winter, but its residents offer a warm welcome. Sights include the Bogdkhan Palace, Choijin Lama Monastery and Museum of Natural History – the latter full of stuffed animals and petrified dinosaur eggs. Since through trains tend to make a prolonged stop at Ulan Bator, travellers who do not plan to alight here will find that this is a good place to stretch their legs and take photos of the train at the station.

South of Ulan Bator, the railway continues its winding journey across the grassy steppes, then crosses the Gobi Desert, where long stretches of straight track make for curious, if somewhat tedious, progress. Gobi simply means 'waterless place or desert', and the desert extends over both Mongolia and China (Inner Mongolia). It is a semi-arid zone with some vegetation that provides an opportunity for Mongolians to graze livestock.

On the evening of day six, the crossing into China requires more bureaucracy at the border post of Dzamin Uud, and then Erenhot (Erlian) in Inner Mongolia. Through trains also need to change bogies on the Chinese side of the desert frontier, where the Russian broad-gauge bogies (1,520 mm/5 ft) are exchanged for those with 1,435 mm (4 ft 8½ in) standard gauge (used by Chinese Railways) for the remainder of the journey. A Chinese locomotive and Chinese dining car are also attached here.

Above The Zuunbayan to Tavantolgoi railway in south-east Mongolia provides access to rich deposits of coal, gold, copper, gypsum and uranium.

Opposite Mining of mostly coal, copper and gold is important to the Mongolian economy, with coal the largest earner, and the railway is used to export this to market. China is the biggest market.

On the morning of day seven, the train passes the mountains of northern China, before pulling into Beijing Main Station in the afternoon.

ATTENTION TO DETAIL

Beijing may be viewed at the end or beginning of the journey, depending on the direction of travel. For those arriving from Moscow, Beijing is a fascinating city and also the departure station for the next leg of a trip by rail to numerous Chinese destinations. China is an intensively rail-connected nation that continues to make enormous investments in new high-speed lines. For dedicated train travellers considering a round trip back to Moscow, there is the option of travelling on the Trans-Manchurian and Trans-Siberian route.

A more difficult but maybe more interesting journey involves returning to Moscow via Urumqi (page 124), and travelling onwards through Astana, the capital of neighbouring Kazakhstan.

SOUTH ASIA

INTRODUCTION

All countries in this part of Asia, except Bhutan and Nepal, have substantive railway networks, although the Afghanistan system is still rudimentary. Nepal Government Railway used to operate a narrow-gauge passenger railway from Janakpur to Siraha and into Jainagar in north-east India. This is now closed, but a broad-gauge railway has been proposed. A link with Bhutan 18 km (11 miles) in length is also planned from Hashimara in West Bengal to Toribari in the landlocked Himalayan kingdom.

With a quarter of the world's population, the other countries – Bangladesh, India, Pakistan and Sri Lanka – have widespread rail networks that are an integral mode of transportation in their respective countries.

The first train to operate in South Asia was in Madras (Chennai) in 1837, while the first passenger train, operating over a distance of 34 km (21 miles) between Bombay (Mumbai) and neighbouring Thane, opened in 1853. This was operated by the Great India Peninsula Railway (GIPR), which later became the Central Railway (CR).

Travelling by train is recommended for most countries in this part of Asia, with India having one of the world's most comprehensive networks.

AFGHANISTAN

The Khyber Pass is a narrow, rocky pass near the border between Afghanistan and Pakistan. It is believed to be one of the world's most strategic mountain passes, offering a direct link from India to Central Asia. Alexander the Great and Mogul emperors recognized its significance, and the British developed a railway in anticipation of transporting troops from Britain to India, despite a train journey of 12 days. In the early 1970s, Afghanistan was an important stop on the overland hippy trail from Europe to Australia. Protracted conflicts basically closed the borders and shut down travel. The Khyber Pass is located in Afghanistan to the east of Kabul and Jalalabad. In the 1970s, the once-a-week '132-Down' train departed from Landi Kotal inside the Pakistani border to Peshawar in western Pakistan. The railway's descent is considered the steepest non-rack-and-pinion line in the world, with safety tracks in the event of runaway trains. Construction began in the 1920s, with the line opening in 1925. It was considered a major engineering feat, involving 92 bridges and culverts, 34 tunnels and four original switchbacks. There are three non-passenger lines in the north and west of Afghanistan, with some connectivity to neighbouring Iran, Turkmenistan and Uzbekistan. Perhaps when peace returns, these lines will be further developed and services on the Khyber Pass may resume.

BANGLADESH

The world's eighth most populous nation, with 164 million people, is well served with 3,600 km (2,200 miles) of rail track. Apart from its border with Myanmar, Bangladesh is surrounded by India and faces the Bay of Bengal. It is a flat country drained by large rivers. The first railway opened as broad track (1,676 mm/5 ft 6 in) in 1862, when it was part of India, and early networks included those of the Bengal Assam Railway. East Pakistan emerged from the partition with India in 1947, and in 1971 became Bangladesh. One of the world's most densely populated nations also has metre-gauge 1,000 mm (3 ft 3 in) track in its eastern part, where its two largest cities of Dhaka and Chittagong are situated. Various trains connect these cities, taking between five and a half and 10 hours, depending on the service. Passengers travel in air-conditioned carriages (sleepers or seats), plus first- and second-class, non-air-conditioned carriages. There are two international services, both to India – *Maitree Express* from Dhaka to Kolkata, and *Bandham Express* from Khulna to Kolkata. These services take about nine hours. Locomotives are diesel (diesel-electric and diesel-hydraulic), plus new Chinese-built, diesel-electric, multiple units. Bangladesh's rail network is expanding.

INDIA

In 1849 the Great Indian Peninsula Railway Company (GIPR) was established, and India's first train departed in 1853 from Bori Bunder, Bombay, to Thane, a distance of 34 km (21 miles). The GIPR was the predecessor of the Central Railway, which eventually became the current Indian Railways.

The world's second most populous nation, with 1.08 billion people, has the world's fourth largest rail network, covering routes of 68,000 km (42,253 miles) in length, 67 per cent of which are electrified. Travelling on the state-owned Indian Railways (one

Above India has one of the most fascinating rail networks in the world, with iconic trains such as those on the Darjeeling Himalayan Railway, being major tourist attractions.

of the world's largest employers) is one of the country's essential travel experiences. Despite its chaotic, bustling appearance, the system is an efficient means of moving hundreds of millions of passengers annually. It is extensive, covering all but the most mountainous terrains. Main lines are either metre gauge 1,000 mm (3 ft 3 in) or broad gauge (1,676 mm/5 ft 6 in), with an increasing number of the former being converted to the latter to enable faster travel. Some mountainous lines, like Darjeeling (page 26) and Shimla (page 30), Nilgiri Mountain Railways from Mettupalayam to Ootacamund, Neral to Matheran, and Pathankot to Jogindernagar, are narrow gauge.

While there are seven classes of travel, the majority of mainline long-distance services offer just five: second-class unreserved; second-class sleeper, and air-conditioned first (AC1), second (AC, two-tier) and third (AC, three-tier). A sheet, blanket and pillow set is recommended for overnight journeys, and is booked separately except on premier trains, where bedding is complimentary. *Shatabdi* (or Century) trains travel during the day, and *Rajdhani Express* (or

Capital City) trains make overnight journeys. Recently, additional fast trains called *Duronto Expresses* (similar to *Rajdhani Express*) have entered service. Other new trains, like *Gatimaan Express* from Delhi to Gwalior and the new *Tejas Express*, are modern versions of the *Shatabdi Express*. The faster and more comfortable trains usually include meals and beverages – they have air-conditioned carriages, and are roomier and less stuffy, with fewer passengers. Windows in second class can be opened to enable closer contact with the countryside and, apart from during the Indian summer, the fresh air ensures traveller comfort. While passengers in the cheaper seats sacrifice comfort, they offer great value for money. Ladies' compartments and ladies' waiting rooms are available on some services, and are patronized by solo female travellers and those travelling with young children.

Most stations are computerized and digital tickets are issued (they can be purchased online or via overseas agents). Each train has its own dedicated name and number, which is useful in locating the departure platform at large stations. Indian trains have a 'foreign tourist quota' that may secure a seat or sleeper even when a train appears to be 'full'. Major stations have dedicated tourist sections to avoid the often lengthy queues used by local travellers.

India has several classic, all-inclusive and expensive trains that convey mostly international tourists in the height of luxury. These include *Palace on Wheels* (page 32), *Deccan Odyssey* (page 38) and the *Maharajas' Express* (India's most luxurious train).

There are international trains to Pakistan, Bangladesh and possibly Nepal. Political tension can, however, affect India to Pakistan services, and travellers need to check their availability in advance.

India's early trains were imported from Britain, but in 1895 the first all-Indian-manufactured steam locomotive left the Ajmer Workshop. The National Rail Museum at Chanakyapuri in New Delhi was established in 1977 as one of 33 museums, heritage parks and galleries managed by Indian Railways. It is open on Thursday to Sunday from 10 a.m. to 5 p.m.

Indian Railways continues to expand its network and upgrade tracks, with speed limits being a major constraint. For example, the *Vande Bharat Express* from New Delhi to Varanasi is India's fastest train, but only hits the design speed of 160 km/h (99 mph) on a short section of its journey of 769 km (478 miles).

PAKISTAN

Trains began operating in what was then part of India in 1855 during the British Raj. The railways were originally local and privately owned, with several amalgamating in 1870 as the Scinde, Punjab and Delhi Railway. More joined the network in 1880 to create the North Western State Railway. With Pakistan's independence in 1947, the Pakistan Western Railway took charge of the tracks.

The network is now operated by the state-owned Pakistan Railways headquartered in Lahore. It manages 7,791 km (4,841 miles) of 1,676 mm (5 ft 6 in) broad-gauge track. The main north–south line is between Peshawar and Karachi (the *Khyber Mail*, page 50) and the principal east–west route is from Rohri to Chaman. Tickets can be purchased for air-conditioned carriages (including sleepers, parlour, business and standard seats), economy class and second-class seats.

Two trains operate between Pakistan and neighbouring India. The *Thar Express* travels between Jodhpur in Rajasthan and Karachi

Above Pakistan's Balochistan Province has 1,470 km (913 miles) of track and passengers trains like the *Jaffer Express* and the *Chaman Passenger.*

in Pakistan, while the *Samjhauta Express* is a passenger service between Delhi and Lahore.

The Quetta (Pakistan) to Zahedan (Iran) line of 732 km (455 miles) runs via Taftan on the Pakistan-Iran border, parallel to the mountains delineating the northern border with Afghanistan. It crosses some of the world's most inhospitable landscapes, described as 'hell upon earth'. Formerly the Trans-Balochistan Railway, it was originally a military link. While its current existence is uncertain, trials have paved the way for a possible Istanbul–Tehran–Islamabad (ITI) rail network extending over 6,500 km (4,030 miles) from Pakistan to Türkiye via Iran.

The Khyber Train Safari (formerly the Khyber Steam Safari) operates a steam locomotive between Peshawar eastwards to Attock Khurd on the Indus River. This is a stretch of the Karachi to Peshawar line, and the tourist train is hauled by Pakistan's only operational steam locomotive.

SRI LANKA

The first Ceylon Government Railways train was introduced by the British in 1864. The first ceremonial run was from Colombo to Ambepussa just north-east of the capital. The first revenue run was in October 1865 from the just-built Colombo Railway Station to Henerathgodde. A line was extended to the Badulla terminus of the highland train in 1924. Its principle function was to transport coffee and tea to Colombo for export. Steam locomotives were used until 1953, when diesel was introduced.

There is now 1,508 km (937 miles) of broad-gauge track (1,676 mm / 5 ft 6 in) throughout the island nation of 22 million people. Trains originate at the capital Colombo on the west coast, radiating out to many points of the compass. The main routes are to the highland tea country, Trincomalee and Batticaloa on the east coast, Galle, Matara and Beliatta to the south, and Jaffna, Mannar and Puttalam in the north. Travellers can expect many serendipitous journeys and experiences on a network that provides gateways to popular sites and attractions.

Historic steam-train and railcar charter trips are offered by

Above The *Viceroy Special* offers a nostalgic and luxurious charter train service to any section of the Sri Lankan rail network.

companies such as JT Tours and Travels. The *Viceroy Special* is a vintage steam train with fully restored period carriages that provide plush seating, as well as a bar, an observation carriage and a dining car where a four-course meal is served. Journeys can be made on any route on the Sri Lanka Railways network, as can those on the *T1 Railcar* (diesel deluxe), a 32-passenger, fully restored, 1940s railcar.

The island's railway history is documented at the Railway Museum near Colombo's Maradana Station.

Many lines have reopened after a protracted and disruptive civil war that extended from 1983 to 2009. Since peace was attained, old railway lines have reopened, new trains have been purchased, and the country now eagerly welcomes tourists. Train journeys offer great value for money and, while slow and usually crowded, they are often more comfortable than those utilizing other transportation modes.

INDIA
DARJEELING HIMALAYAN RAILWAY

THE WORLD'S MOST FAMOUS HILL RAILWAY

The Darjeeling Himalayan Railway (DHR) is a Victorian era narrow-gauge railway masterpiece that was opened in July 1881 between the West Bengal towns of Siliguri and Darjeeling. The line was proposed by Franklin Prestage, an agent for the East Bengal Railway who formed the Darjeeling Steam Railway Company in 1879, when a contract to commence work was written. Its name changed to DHR soon afterwards and has remained ever since.

The railway's connectivity to the outside is Kolkata (Calcutta) some 560 km (348 miles) to the south. There are several daily trains from Kolkata that cover the distance in 8–12 hours, with the *Shatabdi Express* being the fastest day train and the *Darjeeling Mail* an overnight service from Kolkata. The *Radjdhani Express*, from New Delhi to the New Jalpaiguri Junction, has air-conditioned carriages, sleepers and inclusive meals.

Located in the Eastern Himalayas near the Sikkim border, Darjeeling was one of several British hill stations used by senior colonial officials and British troops and their families during the British Raj. They travelled here to escape oppressive summer temperatures on the Bengal Plains. It soon became one of the most appealing and far-flung destinations in the British Empire. Hill stations were developed by colonialists throughout the region – Penang (page 64), Dalat (page 112), Kandy and Nuwara Eliya (page 44) and Bogor (page 60), among others – as holiday destinations, with many being distinctly European in recreating landscapes the colonialists fondly missed.

The railway has operated almost continuously since its inception, and its future was secured in 1999 when it became a UNESCO World Heritage Site. The DHR has changed very little over time, and the quirkiness of its nature and operation has led to its rolling stock being affectionately dubbed 'Toy Trains'.

TRACK NOTES

The railway consists of 88 km (55 miles) of 610 mm- (2 ft-) gauge track between New Jalpaiguri and Darjeeling. It passes through Ghum (Ghoom), India's highest railway station at 2,258 m (7,408 ft), with the increase in altitude from Siliguri to Darjeeling being 1,928 m (6,325 ft).

The line initially started at Siliguri, but in 1964 it was extended to the south to connect with Assam's broad-gauge railway. New

Jalpaiguri developed when the two lines met and is now the largest and busiest junction in India's north-east. On India's independence in 1948, the DHR became part of Indian Railways, and in 1958 it became part of the Northeast Frontier Zone. The line was under continuous threat of closure for years due to high maintenance, particularly during the monsoon, and Indian Railways wanted the service terminated. This threat was lifted in 1999 when it, followed by the Kalka to Shimla Railway (page 30), the Nilgiri Mountain Railways and others, became the Mountain Railways of India UNESCO World Heritage Site. These are just a few of the world's railways to receive such an honour (others protected by UNESCO include Semmering Railway, Austria; Omblin Coal Mining Heritage of Sawahlunto, Indonesia, page 50, and the Rhaetian Railway, Rhätische Bahn, in the Albula/Bernina Landscapes, Italy/Switzerland).

The line is currently worked by steam and diesel locomotives, with one daily, diesel-hauled train in each direction between New

Right The 'Toy Train' operates in Darjeeling on a 610 mm (2 ft) gauge track in the Indian state of West Bengal.

Jalpaiguri and Darjeeling, and one steam-hauled train between Kurseong and Darjeeling. Several tourist trains are also steam worked between Darjeeling and Ghum. The journey from New Jalpaiguri to Darjeeling takes seven hours, but rail enthusiasts could spend several days inspecting the museums and scenic destinations.

Diesel traction was previously provided by two NDM6 Class locomotives supplied new in 2000, and is now provided by six (four were transferred from Matheran), but the real attraction for enthusiasts is the fleet of vintage B Class 0-4-0ST steam engines. These were designed in Britain in the 1880s, with the B Class being a development of the A Class; the first consignment, built by Sharp Stewart in Glasgow, was delivered in 1889.

The major route features, apart from the magnificent scenery, are a unique series of reverses and loops, with the sharpest curve having a radius of 8.8 m (29 ft). These enable the line to climb without tunnels from 100 m (328 ft) above sea level at Siliguri to 2,200 m (7,218 ft) at Darjeeling. Originally there were five loops and six reverses, but flood damage in 1942 and 1991 led to the removal of two loops. The line wages a constant battle with flooding caused by the torrential monsoon rains, and it is a tribute to devoted railway staff that the line is reopened with minimum delay after the rains.

WELCOME ABOARD

The line closely follows the Hill Cart Road of 1869, often running immediately alongside it. This was the road that linked Siliguri with Darjeeling before the railway was built. Its closeness has necessitated the provision of more than 170 level crossings along the shared route (the number varies each time there is a landslip) with the result that, in built-up areas, the route resembles an urban tramway requiring the use of loud horns to warn people.

The railway has its headquarters in Elysia Palace, where the former General Manager's residence is partly a museum. Above Kurseong Station the line runs at a maximum speed of 15 km/h (9 mph) through the bazaar, and is so close to the shops as to be almost part of them. At the dramatically named Agony Point, the carriage overhang gives the impression that the train is riding on air, and passengers were once advised not to leave their seats for a better view in case the train toppled and plunged into the valley.

Ghum station house and yard contain a museum. At certain times of the year it is possible to see the snow-capped peaks of the world's first and third highest mountains: Everest and Kangchenjunga. Such dramatic scenery contributes to many maintaining that this is one of the world's most amazing railway sights. Its charm has resulted in it being the location for Bollywood films including *Jab Pyaar Kisi Se Hota Hai* (1961), *Aradhana* (1969) and *Yaariyan* (2014). Locations in these films have become popular destinations for local tourists. For railway enthusiasts and tourists alike, it is an experience not to be missed.

Darjeeling is popular because of the cooler weather, where it is possible to engage in various activities that are not as taxing as in the hot and humid lowlands. The part Victorian resort and part major tea-growing site sprawls along the ridges of the Darjeeling Hills. A pre-sunrise visit to Tiger Hill to admire the sunrise over the Himalayas is recommended. Kangchenjunga (considered the world's highest peak during the British Raj and a Buddhist sacred site) is normally visible and, on a good day, so is Everest. The Himalayan

Opposite top The driver uses a loud horn to warn pedestrians of the train's approach.

Opposite below Loops and zigzags were built to ease the gradient on Hill Cart Road.

Mountaineering Institution established by Tenzing Norgay, who accompanied Sir Edmund Hillary on the first ascent of Everest, is situated in Darjeeling. Other attractions and activities include a Japanese Gardens, cable car, trekking, paragliding, the Bengal Natural History Museum, Padmaja Naidu Himalayan Zoological Park and the Tibetan Self-help Centre, where handicrafts are sold.

Darjeeling tea is famous around the world and there are some 43,243 acres (17,500 ha) of tea gardens producing 10 million kilograms (22 million pounds) of tea annually. The oldest is Makaibari, dating back to 1859. Most offer tea rooms and shops, and some also provide accommodation. Two well-respected colonial hotels in Darjeeling are Windamere and the Elgin.

Windamere is the original colonial property of Darjeeling, dating back to 1939 and unashamedly retaining elements of the Raj for discerning guests seeking to return to a bygone era. Train enthusiasts will enjoy the luxurious accommodation, expansive landscaped gardens and the DHR Club located in a former stone bungalow. This is the venue in which to meet others fascinated by railways and mountaineering, or to relax in front of the open fire while consulting the extensive library. Historic photos line the wall, and lectures or films often feature here.

ATTENTION TO DETAIL

Numerous services operate on the line, including diesel and steam-hauled locomotives. One daily train operates each way from New Jalpaiguri to Kurseong and Darjeeling (1D and 2D). Buses cover the route more quickly than trains, so the Darjeeling to Ghum service is popular for those with limited time, with 11 daily services between the two upland stations located 30 minutes apart. Known as the Joy Ride, diesel and steam services operate on this route and ticket prices provide complimentary access to the Ghum Railway Museum.

Bookings are advised for this railway and especially the connecting trains to New Jalpaiguri. Two classes of ticket are sold for 1D and 2D, and tickets are slightly more expensive for the more popular Joy Ride steam trains that offer just one class. Various train types are available for charter, ranging from first- and second-class carriages with open windows, to those with air-conditioning, flat wagons and heritage coaches. The seating is simple, with two seats on either side of the aisle, apart from in heritage carriages, which only have one seat on either side of the aisle.

Darjeeling continues to offer relief from India's baking summer temperatures just as it did in the days of the Raj.

KALKA TO SHIMLA

NARROW-GAUGE RAILWAY TO THE FORMER SUMMER CAPITAL

It may not be as famous as the Darjeeling 'Toy Train', but the narrow-gauge Kalka–Shimla Railway (KSR) through parts of the Indian states of Haryana and Himachal Pradesh is one of the world's great mountain railways. In 2008 it was included on the 'Mountain Railways of India' UNESCO World Heritage List. The four and a half hour journey from Kalka in the lowlands to Shimla (also spelt Simla) offers dramatic views, while the journey is truly memorable.

Kalka is situated where the Indo-Gangetic Plain meets the Himalayas. The change in landscape is dramatic and the mountains give reason for Shimla's existence. By 1864 the cool highlands had become the summer capital of the British Raj, and also the headquarters for the British Army in India. Historians note that 20 per cent of the human race was then administered from Shimla. However, links to the outside world were limited and involved long bullock-cart journeys from Calcutta (Kolkata), so a railway was conceived.

TRACK NOTES

The line extends vertically 1,419 m (5,655 ft) from Kalka at 656 m (2,152 ft) to Shimla at 2,075 m (6,806 ft) above sea level. Construction of the 96-km (59-mile), narrow-gauge (762 mm/2 ft 6 in), single-track railway started in 1901, with the line being completed in November 1903.

Establishing the railway especially between Kandaghat and Kanoh Stations was no easy feat. In all, 107 tunnels (only 102 remain and all are numbered, with their lengths painted at their entrances), plus 864 bridges and viaducts, were necessary, with some, like the 'Arch Gallery', being tall and impressive. This arch bridge in three stages was constructed from stone like a Roman aqueduct. When the railway opened, this was the world's highest multi-arch gallery bridge. Bridge No. 226, between Sonwara and Dharampur, is arched, with five-tier galleries of multiple spans, constructed from stone and bridging a deep valley surrounded by high peaks. The longest tunnel is Barog at 1,144 m (3,753 ft).

WELCOME ABOARD

Spectacular scenery and the marvels of the line's construction keep travellers spellbound. The best views are on the right-hand side to Shimla and on the left on the return. Regular trains consist of six small, blue-and-cream coaches hauled by powerful small diesel engines. Tourists can hire a private luxury coach (the *Shivalik Queen*) to attach to the public train, or use the tiny *Himalayan Queen* railcar.

On leaving Kalka, the line meanders through sprawling suburbs before entering the foothills and the climb. The route passes close to the road, crossing it at frequent intervals. It loops back on itself several times at the beginning, using the contours to gain height as it passes through a series of rapidly expanding towns.

The most notable town is Solan, considered to be a mini Shimla. A festival celebrating the goddess Shoolini Devi, after whom the city is named, is staged each summer in June. More materially and perhaps more widely known is the Solan Brewery (India's oldest), which was established by a Briton, Edward Dyer, to brew the famous Lion Beer. It now operates as Kasauli Brewery and is located near Sonwara Station.

Between Solan and Shimla the scenery becomes more rugged and the views become more dramatic. Steep, terraced valleys dominate as the train twists and turns like a snake, burrowing through tunnels or leaping across arched ravines. Passengers can catch their breath (and enjoy a cup of tea) at stations where the train pauses in passing loops before reaching Shimla. Perched on top of a ridge at 1,400 m (4,600 ft), Shimla affords views of the snow-capped Himalayas.

ATTENTION TO DETAIL

The train is operated by the Railway Ministry of the Indian Government. Several trains depart from the Indian capital to connect with those at Kalka for Shimla. The daily morning departure of the *Kalka Shatabdi* from New Delhi connects with the noon train to Shimla for its late-afternoon arrival.

There is an evening sleeper train from Delhi Junction that arrives in Kalka before dawn the following day. Its scheduled time connects with the early morning *Shivalik Deluxe Express* that reaches Shimla by mid-morning (although delays on the *Howrah Kalka Mail* may result in passengers missing the early connection). At selected times (depending on the Operations Department of Northern Railways), the railmotor (an engine that resembles a lorry on tracks) does the Kalka to Shimla section, with the stop in Barog for breakfast being a highlight.

There is a range of accommodation in Shimla, with Chapslee Hotel recommended for those seeking nostalgic accommodation. The landscaped property is nearly 200 years old and is a heritage manor evocative of a bygone era. It was the summer residence of a raja from Punjab, but opened as a mostly original heritage hotel in 1976.

Shimla, sprawling over five hills, is popular with Indian families and honeymooners, and is most crowded in May, June, September and October. The best time to visit is October and November, while snow is common from December to late February.

Above right One of the multi-arched viaducts built with limestone to take the track over difficult terrain.

Right The changeover of trains at Shimla station.

PALACE ON WHEELS

ROMANCE OF THE RAJ

While the time of the British Raj has passed into history, well-heeled travellers can journey on the luxurious *Palace on Wheels* to experience a bygone era, Rajasthan's most impressive heritage cities and picturesque landscapes. Modelled after the famous *Orient Express*, the train starts and finishes in New Delhi, and makes stops in Jaipur, Udaipur, Jaisalmer, Sawai Madhopur (for Ranthambore), Jodhpur, Bharatpur and Agra on its eight-day, all-inclusive journey through the Land of Kings.

This prestigious train was jointly launched in 1982 by Indian Railways and Rajasthan Tourism Development Corporation to help promote Rajasthan. The *Royal Orient* train was later used in Gujarat, but was then discontinued following gauge conversion. *Palace on Wheels* was revitalized and relaunched in 2009.

Originally, many of the saloon carriages were personally owned and used by maharajas who once ruled this part of India. These were sourced and fully restored to their original glory and named after former princely states. As they fell into disrepair, new carriages similar to the originals were constructed. These were run on the metre gauge, with four cabins per carriage and shared shower/toilet facilities. These were subsequently used in Gujarat as the *Royal Orient*, once the gauge-conversion project in Rajasthan occurred. Then a new set of carriages was built for the *Palace on Wheels*, with four cabins per carriage, all with en-suite shower/toilet facilities.

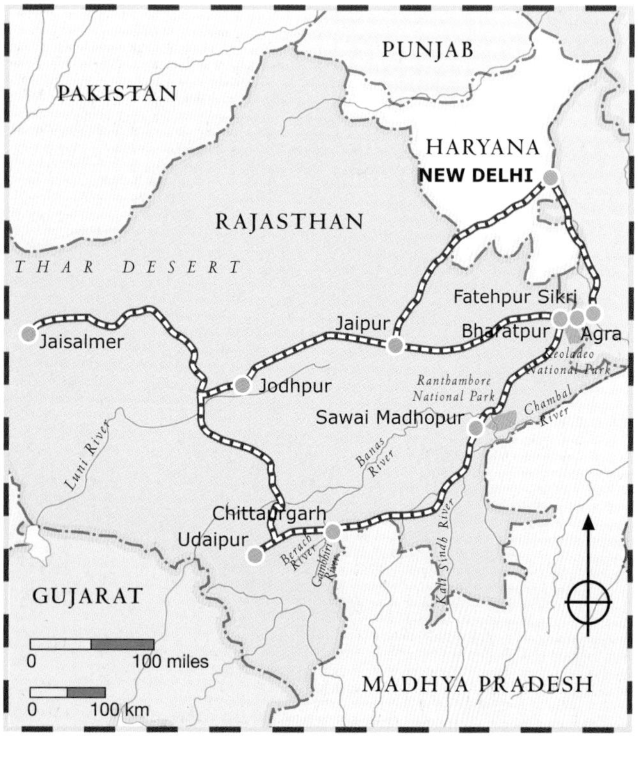

Rajasthan is ideal for train touring, with its old fort cities and semi-desert landscapes. Travelling by luxury train is ideal for well-to-do passengers, who are treated as maharajas and maharanis by staff that delivers personalized service; nothing is left to chance on this slickly managed operation. Passengers equate the train journey to a sea cruise in that once they have checked in and unpacked they do not have to repack for another eight days. Another advantage is that almost everything is covered in the all-inclusive tariff – travel, meals, sightseeing and guides – although personal expenses (beverages, tips, laundry and spa) are additional. The train is noteworthy for its route and destinations, but there are more luxurious Indian trains.

TRACK NOTES

The *Palace on Wheels* was initially a metre-gauge train hauled by a small number of specially prepared steam locomotives, but with steam having largely disappeared from the network by 1995, and with the uni-gauge project having largely replaced metre gauge with broad gauge, the new *Palace on Wheels* is broad gauge. It is usually hauled by a diesel, although a preserved WP Class steam locomotive built by the Baldwin Locomotive Company of Philadelphia in 1947 occasionally appears.

The journey covers 1,860 km (1,156 miles), with most of the travel done in the evening to maximize sightseeing in each destination.

WELCOME ABOARD

Every Wednesday, travellers gather at Delhi's Safdarjung Railway Station in the early evening for their seven-night journey. There is time to inspect their new and lavish home before being seated for a grand dinner as the train heads south to Jaipur.

There are four chambers in each of the 14 carriages, with twin, single or super deluxe (suite) configurations. Wood-veneer panelling with inlaid motifs is a feature, and all chambers have individually

Map showing the route through Rajasthan, with labels: PUNJAB, PAKISTAN, HARYANA, NEW DELHI, RAJASTHAN, THAR DESERT, Jaisalmer, Jaipur, Fatehpur Sikri, Bharatpur, Agra, Jodhpur, Ranthambore National Park, Sawai Madhopur, Chittaurgarh, Udaipur, GUJARAT, MADHYA PRADESH, Luni River, Banas River, Chambal River, 0 100 miles, 0 100 km

Above The *Palace on Wheels* carries a maximum of 82 passengers and has a high staff–passenger ratio to ensure personalized service.

controlled air-conditioning. Each chamber also includes an electronic safe, wi-fi and access to round-the-clock personal assistance from a *khidmatgar*, or assistant. Each carriage has two toilet and shower compartments, plus a mini pantry with a complimentary supply of hot and cold beverages as well as light refreshments. An attached lounge has a television, DVD player and small library.

Other passenger facilities include two restaurants, lounge, well-stocked bar, souvenir shop and spa. The Maharaja and Maharani Restaurants provide formal settings where continental, Chinese, Indian and Rajasthani cuisines are served, although some lunches are taken off the train in iconic locations. Ayurveda treatments, massages and therapies are provided in the spa car. After being acquainted with the facilities and a sumptuous dinner, passengers can enjoy their beverage of choice or retire to their chamber for a restful sleep.

On day two, the train arrives in princely Jaipur in the early morning – this is the gateway city to the vast Thar Desert that extends westwards to the border with Pakistan. Founded in 1727, the capital of Rajasthan, with a population exceeding three million people, is also referred to as India's 'Pink City' due to its numerous dusty and rusty salmon-coloured buildings that change hue with the intensity of light throughout the day. The Hawa Mahal, or 'Palace of Wind', is one such building, with an elegant sandstone facade dominated by filigree windows where the women of the royal household once enjoyed the cooling breezes while discretely watching the outside world. Built in 1799, the palace is part of the Jaipur City Palace complex, with its superb architecture and

Above The train has two dining cars, the Maharaja and the Maharani, which specialize in freshly cooked international cuisine.

Left The ultimate in luxury on the *Palace on Wheels* is one of two super deluxe cabins.

Above Large, panoramic windows allow passengers on the *Palace on Wheels* full views of the ever-changing Indian landscape.

artisan-crafted buildings. Passengers also visit the Albert Hall Museum in the Ram Niwas Gardens, Jantar Mantar and, after lunch, the Amber Fort-Palace and Jaigarh and/or Tiger Fort. At the end of the day, a visit to a bustling bazaar is offered before rejoining the train at Jaipur's Durgapura Station. In Johri Bazaar, visitors are witness to the fact that Rajasthan's history is a living one; it is a place where ancient trades and ornate handicrafts are still practised by contemporary artisans. Bazaars throughout Rajasthan have for centuries been centres of trade and strategic hubs along numerous caravan routes. Successful merchants built lavish residences called havelis, and fort walls were erected to protect the residents and the valuable trades they conducted. Close to the bazaar is one such haveli that has been repurposed as the very smart boutique hotel called Johri.

On day three, passengers awake early for their dawn departure from Sawai Madhopur to Ranthambore National Park for an exhilarating wildlife safari to possibly sight Bengal Tigers, Leopards, Sambar Deer, Marsh Crocodiles and numerous birds, including the Crested Serpent Eagle. While no sightings are guaranteed, it is the excitement of the search that fascinates most visitors, especially photographers.

Back on the train by mid-morning, the journey continues to Chittorgarh, one of Rajasthan's oldest cities, positioned at the confluence of the Gambhiri and Berach Rivers. Here, the Chittorgarh or Chittor Fort, perched on a rocky hill 152 m (499 ft) high above the surrounding city, is the largest fort in India and Asia. Built some 1,300 years ago, it covers an area of 283 ha (700 acres), and features numerous palaces and temples. Along with four other ridge-top forts in Rajasthan, it forms the Hill Forts of Rajasthan UNESCO World Heritage Site.

On day four, Udaipur (City of Lakes) is the next destination. Founded in 1553 and set in the Girwa Valley, surrounded by the Aravalli Hills, lakeside Udaipur is one of Rajasthan's most alluring jewels.

The main attractions passengers experience are the large artificial lake, the Jagdish temple and the fortified City Palace. Passengers are also taken on a tour of the impressive gardens known as Saheliyon-ki-Bari, as well as the Udaipur City Palace with its Crystal Gallery. Lunch is taken in the Shiv Niwas, or

DUNES & DROMEDARIES

Rajasthan is noteworthy for its numerous tribal people, many of them dressed in their brightly coloured clothing. These colours come to the fore at Sam Dunes, where ornately dressed camel herders await to take guests on a memorable camel ride across the extensive dunes. Sunset Dunes with its fairground atmosphere is popular for photography.

While the camels are an important part of the Rajasthani landscape their survival is under threat, with camel numbers seriously declining along with areas for them to graze. Camels are recognized as the state animal and new projects to develop the camel-milk market have given greater value to camels.

In a more easterly part of Rajasthan, the Mela or Pushkar cattle and camel fair staged in November is a riot of colour that could be visited after the *Palace on Wheels* journey. Dedicated camel aficionados can also return to Jaisalmer after their train journey and join a multi-day camel safari into the Thar Desert, stopping at temples and villages like Amar Sagar, Mool Sagar and Bada Bagh while camping out. Safaris vary in price, quality and sightseeing, with four-day treks being the norm.

After refreshments in the desert, passengers are taken back to the train in preparation for a royal dinner enjoyed off the train before returning for the overnight journey to Jodhpur.

Fateh Prakash Hotel, and is followed by a boat excursion on Lake Pichola with its Jag Niwas and Jag Mandir Palaces. Afternoon tea is taken before passengers are returned to the train for its journey of 500 km (311 miles) overnight to Jaisalmer.

On day five, the train arrives in Jaisalmer in Western Rajasthan, near the Pakistani border. Established in 1156, Jaisalmer, or the Golden City, is a desert town along a former caravan route to the Khyber Pass, Central Asia and on to one of the various Silk Road routes between China and Türkiye. The ancient hilltop city fort of Jaisalmer perched on top of Trikuta Hill is clearly visible from the station. Jaisalmer appears as an elevated island in the sea of sand that is the Thar Desert. The old city is protected by fort walls 9 m (30 ft) high, made of thick golden sandstone. Jaisalmer resembles a European medieval city, with its maze of narrow, winding alleyways. Off-train excursions are organized to Gadsisar Lake, Jaisalmer Fort, various Jain temples, Patwon ki Haveli and Nathmal Ji ki Haveli.

After lunch in a hotel, passengers are coached into the surrounding desert wilderness with its extensive sand dunes, oasis villages and camel herds.

On day six, the train arrives in Jodhpur (referred to as the Blue City), retracing the line back to Mandore Railway Station. Passengers wake for a sumptuous breakfast on the train before setting off to explore the Old City, which is a maze of narrow streets protected by a wall 10 km (6 miles) long. Many older buildings have been carved from red sandstone, but others have been painted in a distinctly blue wash – from Mehrangarh Fort rising high above the old walls, the city appears a sea of blue. The colour results from copper sulphate having been added to a limewash used to control the damaging effects of termites. Construction of the fort dates back to 1459, and it remained the royal residence until the grand Umaid Bhawan Palace was completed in 1943.

Umaid Bhawan is one of the largest private residences ever built (it took 3,000 artisans employed over 15 years to complete the palace of 347 rooms). The current maharaja lives in one section of the heritage building with Art Deco detail, while in other parts there is an extensive garden, museum and 70-room luxury hotel currently operated by the Taj Group.

On day seven, the train arrives in Bharatpur for the last full day of off-train touring, covering the four UNESCO World Heritage Sites of Keoladeo National Park in Bharatpur, the deserted city of Fatehpur Sikri, Agra Fort and, of course, the Taj Mahal. The day starts at dawn with a visit to Keoladeo National Park. The

World Wide Fund for Nature (WWF) considers this protected site covering 29 km² (11 sq miles) to be one of the world's best sites for both resident and migratory birds, including the rare Siberian Crane, Greater Spotted Eagle and Imperial Eagle, as well as herons, cormorants, storks and ducks.

After visiting the beautiful city of Fatehpur Sikri, passengers proceed to the majestic Agra Fort, from which they can admire the Taj Mahal at a distance before proceeding to the Taj, which embraces elegance, balance and perfect symmetry on the banks of the Yamuna River. Completed over 23 years from 1630 to 1653, it is considered one of the world's most beautiful buildings. This white-marbled, intricately detailed masterpiece was commissioned by Emperor Shah Jahan as a mausoleum for his wife Arjumand Banu Begum, also known as Mumtaz Mahal.

On day eight, the train arrives back in Delhi, where the journey ends after breakfast on board the train.

ATTENTION TO DETAIL

The train mostly travels through the night and arrives in a new destination as passengers enjoy a leisurely and luxurious breakfast. While many enjoy sleeping with the gentle rocking of the train,

others lament that they miss admiring much of the countryside that the train passes though.

The platform receptions are grand affairs, with colourful groups of locals in traditional clothing accompanied by music and dancing.

The best time to travel is from October to March, thus avoiding the harshness of India's warmer months (April to June) and the following monsoonal rains (July to September). The *Palace on Wheels* only operates between September and April, with tariffs being either peak or lean season as indicated by the train's operator.

Travellers on more modest budgets can plan their own itinerary, using trains of the Indian Railways network to visit all the above destinations on their own journey of discovery through Rajasthan. Individual travellers can also choose to stay in grand hotels such as the Oberoi Amarvilas (Agra), Oberoi Rajvilas (Jaipur), Rambagh Palace (Jaipur), Umaid Bhawan Palace (Jodhpur), Oberoi Udaivilas or Taj Lake Palace (Udaipur). Accommodation in havelis, or merchants' houses, is also available as atmospheric alternatives to conventional hotels.

DECCAN ODYSSEY

THE SPLENDOUR OF MAHARASHTRA

Based on the success of the *Palace on Wheels* (page 32), the *Deccan Odyssey* luxury train was introduced in early 2004 as a collaboration between Indian Railways and the State Government of Maharashtra, and recently with the operation and catering being coordinated by Zalika Enterprises.

While marketed as the *Deccan Odyssey*, this service actually offers six unique itineraries to various parts of the Indian states of Maharashtra, Rajasthan, Gujarat and Karnataka. Each journey has a unique name, and offers a snapshot of the iconic and cultural attractions of its various journeys through Western India. The six journeys are Maharashtra Splendour, Indian Odyssey, Jewels of the Deccan, Indian Sojourn, Hidden Treasures of Gujarat and Maharashtra Wild Trail.

The following description is for the eight-day, seven-night Maharashtra Splendour journey, which begins and ends in Mumbai (previously Bombay), the Maharashtra capital and India's largest city, with some 12.5 million residents.

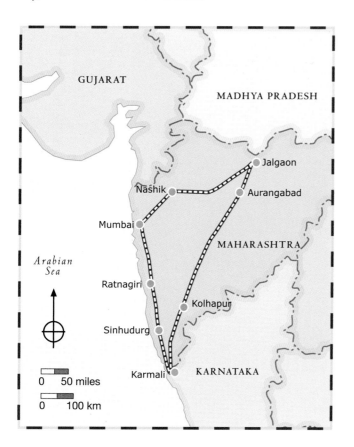

Like the *Palace on Wheels*, these journeys cater mostly to affluent foreign travellers who appreciate checking in, unpacking and enjoying eight days of deluxe facilities, personalized service, and the opportunity to explore several dispersed and wondrous sights in the form of all-inclusive fares covering train travel, accommodation, meals and off-train excursions, plus entry fees to iconic sites along the way, and only packing their bags once at the end of the trip. Tariffs exclude applicable taxes, personal laundry and alcoholic beverages.

TRACK NOTES

The train's first commercial run was flagged off in February 2004 and it now operates for 35 weeks of the year, avoiding the Indian summer. Interestingly, India's first passenger train travelled just 35 km (22 miles) from what was then Bombay's Victoria Station (now Mumbai's Chhatrapati Shivaji Terminal) to Thane in 1853. The railway station in southern Mumbai and close to the Arabian Sea is one of the grandest in the world. It is recognized as a UNESCO World Heritage Site for its Victorian Gothic facade that remains architecturally authentic and mostly unchanged since its construction in the late nineteenth century.

The carriages of the *Deccan Odyssey* were fitted out by the Integral Coach Factory in Perambur near Chennai (formerly Madras). The locomotive is capable of speeds of 110 km/h (68 mph) but mostly moves at a more respectable speed of just 80 km/h (50 mph). Trains of the *Deccan Odyssey* share the line with regular services of the Indian Railways network.

WELCOME ABOARD

With the opening of the Suez Canal in the 1860s, Mumbai became the principal maritime gateway to the subcontinent. Mumbai is also the home of Bollywood, the world's biggest film industry. The Taj Mahal Palace Hotel, considered one of the grandest hotels in the world, has appealed to discerning travellers since its completion in 1903. Located in Colaba District facing the Arabian Sea, Mark Twain called it 'a bewitching place, a bewildering place, an enchanting place'. The Old Wing is the section in which to be seen, while the newer Tower Wing built in 1973 is more luxurious but without the history. The Gateway of India (an arched

Above The *Deccan Odyssey* is a luxury Indian train that operates six different itineraries from its base in Maharashtra state.

monument built to welcome King George V and Queen Mary in 1911) adjoins the hotel.

Arriving early to take in the architecture, grandeur and congestion that is Mumbai's main railway station is worth considering. There is also an information and booking counter here for Maharashtra Tourism. UNESCO notes the significance of the stone cathedral-like dome, turrets, pointed arches and eccentric ground plan that makes the station so important to global culture. Its architecture resembles that of a traditional palace, and celebrates the English architect Frederick Stevens and the skilled local artisans who put his plan into practice. This successful union of skills is similar to those that went into the construction of Kuala Lumpur's historic old railway station in the Malaysian capital (page 64). It is worth noting that the station in Mumbai is fully functional, with an

estimated three million commuters passing through it every day, making it one of the world's busiest transport hubs. A scene from the Oscar-winning film *Slumdog Millionaire* (2008) was filmed here.

Passengers assemble at Mumbai's Chhatrapati Shivaji Terminal on Saturday afternoon for this journey of discovery through Maharashtra's hinterland and into the Western Ghats. The Western Ghats mountain range runs for 1,600 km (990 miles), parallel to much of India's West Coast. It too was recognized by UNESCO as a World Heritage Site in 2012, and it is also a hotspot for biological diversity. The range has an average elevation of 1,200 m (3,900

ft), and is ecologically significant in that it prevents the south-west monsoon from reaching the Deccan Plateau.

The *Deccan Odyssey* carries a maximum of 80 guests, who are accommodated in air-conditioned, two-berth deluxe cabins split into five deluxe doubles and 31 deluxe twins (referred to by the train's operator as coupes), or presidential suites. One cabin has been modified to accommodate those with limited mobility. The train has 21 carriages, including 11 for accommodation, one conference car, two restaurant cars, one Ayurvedic spa car, one bar/lounge car, and five cars for staff, luggage and generators. The conference car offers television, a small library and a business centre. The spa car has two treatment rooms, plus a sauna, beauty parlour and mini gym.

Nine carriages accommodate well-furnished deluxe cabins, with another two dedicated to just four presidential suites (two per car). Every deluxe cabin carriage has four twin-bed cabins of 8.8 m² (95 ft²) each, plus a small lounge at one end of the carriage. These deluxe cabins have two beds, and a shower, sink and toilet with all amenities. The four presidential suites are 19 m² (205 ft²) each with a double bed, separate sitting room, sofa, desk and two

bathrooms. Guests travelling in the presidential suites also receive complimentary drinks from the bar, free laundry and private-car sightseeing with their own dedicated driver and guide.

After unpacking, meeting fellow passengers and their personal car attendant, and inspecting the train's facilities, it is time for the passengers to prepare for pre-dinner drinks and dinner. Three daily meals are provided in the tariff, with most taken on the train in one of two restaurant cars, where gourmet western, oriental, Indian and continental meals are served, mostly prepared from fresh ingredients obtained from destinations along the way.

Following breakfast on day two, the train pulls into Nashik, where passengers alight for a stroll along the Godavari Ghats and to observe Hindus performing religious rituals. Nashik is also becoming increasingly popular with those who enjoy wine. Some 66 per cent of India's burgeoning wine industry is focused on Maharashtra State, and about half of the country's wine estates are located near Nashik. Wine is also produced near Bangalore and in the Indian states of Himachal Pradesh (Shimla and Kullu), Karnataka and Andhra Pradesh. Some of the celebrated Nashik wineries include Vallonne, Sula and the French Champagne house

Above Peshwa I and Peshwa II restaurants on the train offer Indian, oriental and continental cuisines.

Right Cabins in one of 12 accommodation coaches on the train have modern fittings and round-the-clock service is provided.

Opposite Passengers can relax over a drink and a good book or share travel tales with fellow travellers.

Chandon, where well-known international grape varieties like Shiraz, Cabernet Sauvignon, Sauvignon Blanc, Chenin Blanc, Zinfandel, Merlot and Pinot Noir are grown for the production of table and sparkling wines.

Passengers are transferred to Grover Zampa Vineyards in the Nashik Valley for a winery tour, followed by a sumptuous lunch paired with the estate's finest wines that could include the sparkling Zampa Soirée, a single vineyard Shiraz under the Insignia label and a late harvest Viognier Vendages Tardives. After a leisurely lunch, it is back to the train for the next leg of the journey.

After a reception from musicians at Aurangabad on the third morning, passengers are transferred by coach to Ellora, some 29

Above The Indian Odyssey travels through fabled landscapes to landmark destinations in the ultimate of luxury.

km (18 miles) away. The surrounding district is a centre of Mughal culture, and this UNESCO site is considered one of India's finest examples of cave-temple architecture. The mausoleum Bibi Ka Maqbara was built as a replica of the Taj Mahal. Ellora Caves has some 100 caves – with 34 open to the public – cut into a basalt ridge at the heart of the Deccan Plateau to showcase Buddhist, Jain and Hindu art. There are 12 Buddhist caves to the south, 17 Hindu caves in the centre and five Jain caves to the north. They date back from the seventh to the tenth centuries and feature art from all three religions, with the Jain and Hindu art dating back at least 1,600 years. Some caves feature ornate frescoes and intricate architectural detailing, with cave 16 being the most celebrated site of Kailash Temple, believed to be a replica of Lord Shiva's celestial abode on Mount Kailash.

Following lunch back on the train, time is allocated to rest and relax while the train departs for its next destination. The journey from Aurangabad to Ajanta for the activities on day four is just a short one of 100 km (60 miles). Alighting at Jalgaon Station, the day's main activity is journeying 58 km (36 miles) to Ajanta Caves. This UNESCO-recognized site features 30 Buddhist temples chiselled from basalt cliffs and dating back some 2,650 years. They were mostly forgotten about until the nineteenth century, and this 'neglect' may account for their excellent condition and preservation. The intricate cave temples (*chaitya*s) and monasteries (*vihara*s) were hand-hewn from near-vertical sides of a horseshoe-shaped ravine above the Waghora River.

Lunch and dinner are taken on board as the train heads for the colourful city of Kolhapur. On the fifth morning, the train rolls into Kolhapur on the banks of the Panchaganga River. Passengers disembark for a city tour that includes the 1,300-year-old Mahalakshmi Temple and the New Palace Museum, a beautiful octagonal palace built in 1884. The Town Hall Museum is visited before shopping at the local market. Later, passengers enjoy refreshing afternoon tea in a special venue, where a folk performance and traditional martial arts display is staged. In the late afternoon, passengers return to the *Deccan Odyssey* for dinner and its departure for day six in Goa.

If it is Thursday, it must be Goa. After breakfast on the train, passengers alight at Madgaon Station to explore India's smallest state. Goa was a Portuguese colony from 1510 to 1961, when it reverted back to Indian control. The Portuguese made a lasting impression on the local culture, cuisine and architecture, like they did in other parts of Asia such as Melaka (Malacca) and Macau.

Sightseeing in Goa includes being driven to Fontainhas, the Latin Quarter in Panjim, with the well-preserved Portuguese-style housing on this site recognized by UNESCO. There is time to walk around Fontainhas, with its winding alleyways adorned by tiled roofed houses in decorative shades of red and blue. Then it is time to visit the Goan capital Ribandar, and to enjoy a walk taking in its ancient churches and the ruins of the St Augustine Tower. Afterwards, passengers are driven to the Sahakari Spice Plantation for lunch, which includes dishes with Hindu origins, but which are infused with Portuguese culinary traditions dating

back 400 years. Guests enjoy shrimp, kingfish and mackerel plus *feni*, a potent liquor made from cashew nuts. After lunch, there is a folk performance and a tour of the spice plantation. On the way back to the train, time is taken to inspect a traditional Goan house. In the late afternoon, passengers return to the train to prepare for dinner as the train heads to Sindhudurg. The route taken through the Konkan Region in the afternoon and early evening is considered one of the most scenic of the whole journey. The view includes the Arabian Sea to the west and Sahyadri Hills in the east. The line is considered a marvellous feat of engineering through the seemingly insurmountable hills.

The train arrives at Ratnagiri Station on the seventh morning and from here, passengers are transferred to Sindhudurg, which lies on a rocky island just off the coast. The fort was built in the seventeenth century to counter the rising interest that European powers had in this part of the subcontinent facing the Arabian Sea. After admiring the fort, covering 19.5 ha (48 acres), passengers visit Pinguli Village, the local museum and the decorative Sawantwadi Palace built in the eitghteenth century. Here lunch of local Malvani cuisine is enjoyed. Back on the train, dinner is served as the overnight journey of 450 km (280 miles) back to Mumbai begins.

After breakfast on the eighth day, the train arrives back in Mumbai, where passengers alight at the end of their thrilling adventure.

ATTENTION TO DETAIL

The train is operational from September to May, and berths are sold as single or double occupancy for both the deluxe cabins and the presidential suites. At other times, the train is available for charter services. Five-star services offered and meals served are overseen by staff from Zalika Enterprises.

Passengers on associated *Deccan Odyssey* trains can explore other Indian cities and iconic sites like Jaipur, Agra, Udaipur, Jodhpur, Jaisalmer and Kutch. Bookings can be made directly with the train, or via leading global travel services such as Indian Luxury Trains in the UK.

The *Deccan Odyssey* provides a wonderfully relaxed way to experience the culture, beauty and history of a vibrant part of India. It offers six meticulously conceived journeys, all lasting seven nights and eight days. All the journeys depart from Mumbai, apart from the Indian Odyssey, which starts at Delhi and ends in Mumbai.

SRI LANKA
COLOMBO TO KANDY & TEA COUNTRY

GATEWAY TO THE TEA HIGHLANDS

Sri Lanka has shrugged off the devastation of its civil war (the conflict lasted 30 years and ended in 2009) and reopened long-closed railway lines to provide a wonderful opportunity to explore the island's picturesque and colourful landscapes. Trains originating from the capital Colombo head to various parts of the island, including north to Jaffna and Mannar, easterly to Batticaloa and Trincomalee, and to Beliatta on the south coast (page 46). There is a commuter service linking Colombo with Negombo and Puttalam.

Trains are comfortable, mostly with two classes and some with an additional first class. Third class offers great value for money but the wooden benches are normally crowded; second class has padded seats and fans and is less crowded, while first class has air-conditioned coaches, observation saloons and sleeping berths on some trains.

TRACK NOTES

A popular route is to Kandy and the highlands where the famous Ceylon tea is grown. The line from the current capital to the former capital of Kandy was built between 1858 and 1868 in what was then Ceylon. It was extended through what is known as tea country to the terminal at Badulla, with the journey taking approximately 10 hours.

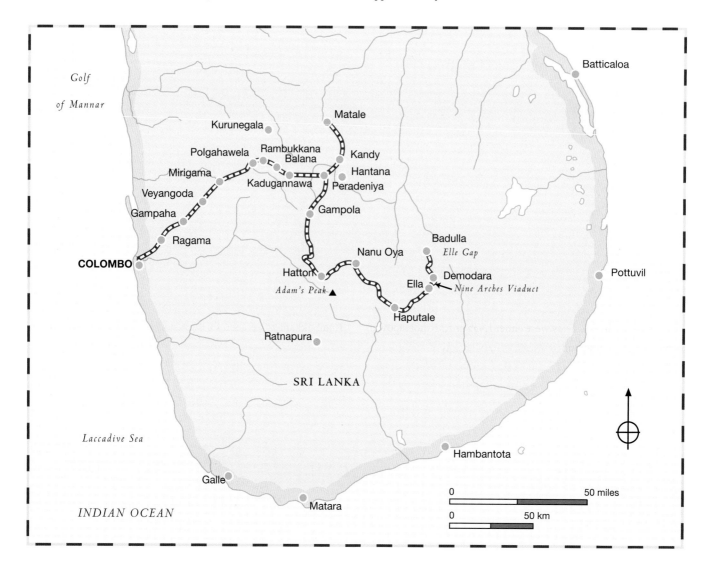

The train from Colombo to Badulla was hauled on some sections by two steam engines – one in the front and another at the rear to provide surer braking and greater thrust. The *Udarata Menike* was introduced in 1956 and powered by two British diesel locomotives hauling new sets of carriages. Twelve Canadian diesel locomotives were also introduced in the 1950s and '60s under the Colombo Plan as a gift from the Canadian government. These diesel locomotives, named Alberta, Montreal, Saskatchewan, Prince Edward Island, Vancouver, Manitoba, Toronto and Ontario, had their names painted on either side of each locomotive gleaming in silver-and-blue livery. They were either 1,435 or 1,310 horsepower locomotives. Chinese-built S12 class trains were introduced in 2012, while S14-class trains came into service in 2019 and are now used to operate a service between Colombo and Badulla.

Today, several daily trains make the journey from Colombo to Badulla, stopping at major stations such as Kandy, Ella, Haputale and Nana Oya. They pass a variety of landscapes, with the highlights being tea plantations, waterfalls and steep escarpments.

WELCOME ABOARD

The train travels inland from Colombo past rice fields on either side of the track to Polgahawela Junction, where the lines to the

Above A heritage Sri Lankan train passing through Holyrood Estate in the Talawakelle-Nanu Oya tea-growing district operated by the famous Dilmah Ceylon Tea Company.

north diverge and the climb to Kandy begins. From here the scenery changes, the rice fields are left behind and the hilly countryside appears from what is now a single-track line.

A rising gradient of 1 in 44 dominates the climb to Kadugannawa at 520 m (1,700 ft) above sea level. This height is best appreciated from Balana, where Sensation Curve, a sheer precipice of 300 m (984 ft), is just outside the train window. The section from Rambukkana to Peradeniya is considered one of the most picturesque sections of railway in Sri Lanka, and passengers are advised to sit on the right-hand side while the train climbs the mountain to make the most of the dramatic views, and the numerous sharp curves and steep drops. After this, the last stretch of the journey to Kandy is almost anti-climactic. Some may alight to inspect the extensive Royal Botanic Gardens located at Peradeniya west of Kandy. The gardens were established by the British and contain many rare plants.

The line branches at Peradeniya Junction, with the southern route heading towards Badulla, while the northeastern line continues to Kandy. The recommended route is to travel to Kandy, spend some time there, then join a train for Badulla. Kandy is located in the centre of the island on a plateau at an altitude of 500 m (1,640 ft), 121 km (75 miles) from Colombo.

Many travellers to Kandy visit the famous Dalada Maligawa, or the Temple of the Tooth, housing what is understood to be a tooth of Buddha. Popular with pilgrims, the relic is housed in a fourth-century gold casket. Esala Perahera, staged in July or August, is a 10-day Buddhist festival involving a procession with the relic carried on the back of a decorated elephant preceded by a vibrant parade of dancers and drummers. The Pinnewala Elephant Orphanage located to the west of Kandy is worth visiting at other times of the year.

Hatton is a popular stop, especially for pilgrims who alight here to climb Adam's Peak (Sri Pada Mountain) at 2,243 m (7,358 ft), some 30 km (18.6 miles) away. Most people start climbing from the Dalhousie trailhead at 2.30 a.m., following the illuminated trail comprising 5,500 steps, to arrive at the summit for sunrise. The seven-hour return journey is not for the faint-hearted. January and February are the pilgrimage months, when the train becomes crowded, while April is the season to visit Nuwara Eliya and a good time to avoid for those who do not enjoy crowds.

Others alight here to stay in former planters' residences on tea estates to enjoy a nostalgic and elegant colonial experience.

Alight from the train at Nanu Oya Station, 8 km (5 miles) from Nuwara Eliya, to spend time enjoying old clubs like the Hill Club and hotels such as the Windsor, St Andrew's and the Grand Hotel. All provide an insight into a bygone era, when holidaying options were limited. Once referred to as Little England, mountainous areas such as Nuwara Eliya offer cooler weather and a respite from the lowland heat. Guests can expect heavy wooden furniture, stuffed hunting trophies, billiard rooms, mosquito nets and refined afternoon teas.

Recreational activities are more pleasant in the cooler mountains, with Nuwara Eliya at 1,868 m (6,128 ft) altitude appealing as a destination for walking, golf and tennis. Temperate flowers, fruits and vegetables flourish around the town centred on Gregory Lake and Victoria Park. District attractions include Horton High Plains National Park (World's End), Sri Pada Wilderness Sanctuary, Galway's Land National Park (for birdwatching), and Hakgala Botanic Gardens, which is famous for orchids and roses.

Express trains only stop at a few other stations, including Haputale, the 69th station from Colombo. The town is surrounded by hills, cloud forests and tea plantations, and the stop provides access to several popular natural areas. Lipton's Seat at Dambetenna in the Haputale Range is a lookout named after Sir Thomas Lipton, one of the pioneers associated with Ceylon tea.

One hour before reaching Badulla the train stops at Ella, where there are dramatic views of the southern plains from Elle Gap. The train terminates at the provincial capital Badulla, 292 km (182 miles) from Colombo. This service town perched at 680 m (2,230 ft) above sea level is surrounded by tea estates and provides access to natural adventures in Horton High Plains National Park and Knuckles Conservation Forest.

ATTENTION TO DETAIL

Tickets for this route can be purchased from counter numbers two and eight at Colombo Fort Station. A first-class seat in a classic observation car is the seat many travellers prefer to book. These 24-seater cars are at the rear of the train with the seats facing backwards. The open windows are considered a plus, especially by photographers. The tickets need to be purchased in advance, usually from private agents.

Chinese-built S14 class trains, introduced in 2019, operate the daily *Denuware Menike* service between Colombo, Kandy, the highlands and Badulla. These diesel-electric, multiple-unit trains were financed by a Chinese sovereign loan. Nine diesel sets have been supplied by CRRC Qingdao Sifang, China. While only the two first-class cars are air-conditioned, the other carriages have windows that can be opened, and doors are often left open to cool the interiors.

There is a night train from Colombo to Badulla that travels via Peradeniya Junction and therefore does not connect to Kandy. The train departs the capital at 8 p.m. and arrives in Badulla at 7.10 a.m. One car has two-berth bunk sleeping compartments, but these get booked early. Sleeperette seating with greater recline than normal seating is available in the other two classes. The Badulla to Colombo night sleeper mail train departs at 10.46 p.m. and arrives in Colombo at 5.17 a.m. the following morning.

One idiosyncrasy of Sri Lankan trains is that most coaches have seats labelled 'reserved for clergy'. Otherwise, reservations can be made for first class but not second and third. Buffet compartments are available on the main express trains, and hawkers sell snacks and drinks at station stops.

Right The 25-m (80-ft) high stone and concrete arches, considered a major feat of architecture and construction, are a popular attraction for train aficionados.

COLOMBO TO MATARA

SOUTH COAST LINE

The line heads south from Colombo to Galle and continues on to Matara before terminating at Beliatta, 40 minutes east of Matara. Several daily trains, including the *Udarata Menike*, grip the coast for much of the journey, although Beliatta is located inland.

In parts, the track is so close to the coast that spray enters the carriages through open windows. On 26 December 2004 this line became infamous for the worst rail disaster in history when a tsunami associated with an earthquake off Aceh (Indonesia) washed the *Matura Express* from the rails near Peraliya. Some 1,700 people perished, mostly by drowning as waves 7 m (29 ft) tall swept locomotive 591 Manitoba and its carriages away.

TRACK NOTES

Ironically, the line is considered to be one of the world's most scenic, as it travels at sea level with picturesque beaches on one side and forest on the other.

New Chinese-built S14 units operate a daily service. Each train has two 74-tonne (81.5-ton) power cars with a 1,950 hp, MTV, 12V, 4,000 R41 diesel engine, plus seven intermediate coaches. There are two first-class air-conditioned coaches with a capacity of 88 passengers, two second-class cars to accommodate 96, and three third-class cars accommodating 216. Other features include a dining compartment and toilets that provide disabled access.

Train traditionalists will miss the rear observation saloon of the *Udarata Menike*, which has been removed with the introduction of these units.

WELCOME ABOARD

Many south-bound trains depart from Colombo's Maradana Station before passing the National Railway Museum and arriving at Colombo Fort Station. Because these trains are popular, it is advisable to join the train at Maradana to guarantee a seat, as most passengers board at Colombo Fort. The right-hand side of the train – and the opposite on the return journey – secures the best sea views to Matara. Within minutes of passing Galle Face Green and the famous Galle Face Hotel, the train turns south to follow the coast. The hotel is perfect for those seeking a grand colonial-style property, afternoon teas on its wide verandahs facing the sea and the opportunity to relive a golden era of travel. Beach resort towns soon appear, with Hikkaduwa a destination popular for its beaches and turtle watching.

Galle is a historic port first encountered by Europeans when the Portuguese arrived in the early sixteenth century and named it Santa Cruz. The Dutch seized control in 1640, and in 1663 added to the hexagonal-shaped fort located on a wide bay 119 km (74 miles) from Colombo. The British seized control in 1796, and remained in control until independence in 1948. Galle is considered Asia's largest and finest remaining European fort city. The historic town is protected by high walls and thick ramparts, and with the Old Town of Galle and its Fortifications, is a UNESCO World Heritage Site. The city is home to more than 100,000 residents, with many living and working within the confines of the fort, which extends over 52 ha (128.5 acres). Hotels, restaurants and residences, along with attractions like the National Maritime Archaeological Museum, Lighthouse, Fort Clocktower, Historical Mansion Museum and Dutch Reformed Church, are located within the fort.

The railway from Galle to Matara hugs the coast, passing palm-fringed beaches, lagoons and villages, with most accessible by train. These include Unawatuna, Weligama and Mirissa, with a variety of accommodation, including several luxurious resorts that are accessible from Kumbalgama Station. Whale and dolphin watching tours are conducted from Mirissa (alight at Polwathumodara or Mirissa Station). Stilt fishermen (known in Sinhalese as *ritipanna*) can be seen along the foreshore near Koggala Station.

Matara, 160 km (100 miles) from Colombo, is a major coastal city featuring historical attractions from the Dutch and British eras, as well as temples, pagodas and a lively market at Nupe Junction. Five daily trains operate between Matara and Beliatta. Yala National Park is an essential venue for nature lovers and those seeking photographs of wildlife like Asian Elephants, Leopards and birds.

ATTENTION TO DETAIL

There are several daily trains, although some departures are on specific days and some terminate at Galle or Matara. Train 8040 is a daily through service from Kandy to Colombo and on to Matara (departing at 5.10 a.m., arriving at noon), while Train 8039 does the journey in reverse (departing at 1.40 p.m., arriving at 8.58 p.m.). All offer third- and second-class seating, while just one daily train from Colombo to Beliatta and return offers first class on the Chinese-built unit with its distinctive blue livery.

Vintage steam trains operated as the *Viceroy Special* also make journeys along the southern route. The operator additionally operates a T1 Railcar (diesel deluxe), which can accommodate 32 passengers in a fully restored, 1940s railcar.

While influenced by the monsoon, Sri Lanka is a year-round destination as there is always some part least affected by rain. The best time to visit the south and west, and the hill country, is from December to April.

Below A diesel-electric railcar is available for charter by the operators of the *Viceroy Special*.

KARACHI TO PESHAWAR

KHYBER MAIL

A railway once traversed the strategic Khyber Pass between Pakistan and Afghanistan. The mere mention of the Khyber Pass conjures up an exotic journey for many railway enthusiasts, but for now the line, 64 km (40 miles) in length, from Peshawar to Landi Kotal at 1,065 m (3,494 ft) above sea level, is closed due to landslides and political instability. The pass was the most direct link between India and Central Asia, a fact not lost on many, including Alexander the Great and the British who once ruled here. The British-built, wide-gauge line was opened in 1925 and was then the world's steepest non-rack railway. Its primary function was militaristic, while safety tracks were installed to divert runaway trains. Two locomotives were used to negotiate the switchbacks, and the now-closed section into Afghanistan is considered an engineering marvel.

Pakistan impresses for its scenery, culture, food and fertile floodplains extending from the Himalayas to Karachi on the Arabian Sea. Historic mountain passes, including the Karakoram Highway through to Kashgar, provide access to China, although not all connections are permanently open.

However, the Main Line (ML-1) of 1,687 km (1,048 miles) from Karachi to Peshawar is open, with several trains operated by Pakistan Railways using all or sections of the track. Pakistan's most important line was built in five stages between 1861 and 1900, and is currently being upgraded as part of the China–Pakistan Economic Corridor. Double tracking will double current train speeds to 160 km/h (100 mph).

The first line built was the Karachi to Kotri section of 1,676 mm (5 ft 6in), and the last from Lahore to Peshawar, including the well-fortified Attock Bridge over the Indus River, was completed in 1883.

TRACK NOTES

This line connects the cities of Karachi, Lahore, Rawalpindi ('Pindi'), Islamabad and Peshawar, and while there are 184 stations most trains only stop at a few. The *Khyber Mail* departs Karachi at 10 p.m. on day one and arrives in Peshawar at 6.30 a.m. on day three.

At Rohri, the line to the north-west for Sibi and Quetta branches from the main line after crossing the Indus River between Rohri and Sukkar. This bridge was completed in 1889 to replace steam ferries that transported carriages across the river. Carriages of emerald-green-and-cream livery are hauled by diesel locomotives.

WELCOME ABOARD

The *Khyber Mail* departs Karachi to connect to Islamabad and on to the border city of Peshawar. The former capital Karachi, with 15 million residents, has attractions including Chaukhandi Tombs, Mohatta Palace, Empress Market and Port Grand.

Hyderabad, on the Musi River, is the first stop. Those who alight can admire Golconda Fort, Charminar, Taj Falaknuma Palace, Birla Mandir and pearl shops, and enjoy Hyderabadi cuisine.

The train originally crossed the Indus River via the Lansdowne Bridge between Rohri and Sukkur. It now adjoins the Ayub Bridge built in 1962, which the train crosses.

Passengers alighting at Lahore can admire Lahore Fort (eleventh century), Shalimar Gardens (UNESCO World Heritage Site), Badshahi Mosque, Food Street and Liberty Market. Lahore is just kilometres from the Wagah border crossing for Amritsar, where nationalistic displays by Indian and Pakistani guards are of interest to visitors.

The nation's planned capital, Islamabad, contrasts with its older twin city, Rawalpindi. The latter has numerous heritage buildings, including havelis, temples and Rohtas Fort.

Above The Lansdowne Bridge over the Indus River in Sukkur is considered one of the great engineering feats of the 19th century and is the largest cantilever bridge ever built.

Trains pass the Golra Sharif Railway Museum just south-east of Taxila – one of the world's oldest continuously populated cities, with Buddhist relics that predate Islam. With three halls and an extensive yard, the museum includes British Raj relics (from North West Railways, as the network was called before Pakistan's 1947 independence), a saloon car used by India's Viceroy, Lord Mountbatten, and another belonging to the Jodhpur Maharaja. There are visions for a nostalgic steam-train journey through Pakistan.

The *Khyber Mail* terminates at Peshawar Cantonment. Peshawar was once encircled by defensive walls with 16 gates protecting the market town as viewed from the train, or Qissa Khwani Bazaar when the train has reached its destination.

The Khyber-Pakhtunkhwa Province is recovering from a post-militancy environment, and visitors should inquire about the possible reopening of the Peshawar to Landi Kotal Line.

ATTENTION TO DETAIL

Trains have various classes, with those recommended for long journeys being air-conditioned sleepers. Other classes include first-class sleeper, air-conditioned lower class (seats and sleepers), parlour car (for short journeys), economy class and second class (seats and sleepers). Air-conditioned carriages can be cold, while other carriages have fans plus windows that open. Most trains have a restaurant car, but passengers should bring their own food.

Station facilities are functional but limited in infrastructure and services. The website for Pakistan Railways is problematic and trains do not always run punctually, so prepare to be flexible. Technically, tickets can only be purchased by Pakistani nationals and online purchases using local credit cards, so it is a good idea to seek agent assistance. Trains are popular with Pakistan's 221 million citizens and can be crowded during holidays. Plan travel carefully as summers can be blistering hot, while winter nights can be cold.

SOUTHEAST ASIA

INTRODUCTION

Railways exist in all Southeast Asian nations except Brunei, with Cambodia and the Philippines having limited connections. Trains are popular and offer value for money, but get crowded during holidays. There are some international connections, like those between Malaysia and Thailand plus Vietnam and China. The *Eastern & Oriental Express* (page 74) traverses Singapore, Malaysia and Thailand.

The regional rail landscape is ever changing, and China's evolving Belt and Road Initiative has opened new routes from China into the region. This initiative involves massive infrastructure extending through 70 countries, with high-speed, dual-track lines proposed for Thailand, Lao PDR, Vietnam, Myanmar and Cambodia.

BRUNEI DARUSSALAM

While Brunei no longer has railways, its first line from Brooketon Coal Mine to Muara opened in the1880s. Initially a wooden tramline, steel rails were added in the 1890s to enable steam locomotives to run on the 711 mm (2 ft 4 in) gauge. The mine and railway closed in 1924. In the 1930s, Royal Dutch Shell laid a 600 mm (2 ft) railway between Seria Refinery and Badas. It was dismantled during the Second World War and rebuilt in 1945, but discontinued in the early twenty-first century. A liquefied natural gas plant in Lumut incorporates a 1,533 mm (5 ft 3 in) railway along a pier.

Below The recently opened Jakarta to Bandung High Speed Rail Line is a major infrastructure investment under China's Belt and Road Initiative.

CAMBODIA

The French laid tracks in the 1930s, when Cambodia was within French Indochina. Some 612 km (380 miles) of 1,000 mm (3 ft 3 in) gauge track is currently laid and in various states of repair on the Southern Line (Phnom Penh to Sihanoukville) and the North-west Line (Phnom Penh to Poipet). Railways were disrupted during the Khmer Rouge era (1975–1979) but are being rebuilt. The Southern Line enables travel between Phnom Penh and Sihanoukville port, and destinations like Kampot (page 56). Services are operated by the privately owned Cambodia Royal Railways.

There are no international railways into Cambodia, but this could change along a possible route from Aranyaprathet / Ban Khlong Luk (Thailand), through Phnom Penh, to Ho Chi Minh City (Vietnam). Should this open, the line will enable direct travel from Singapore all the way to Karskaya (Russia), the world's northernmost station.

INDONESIA

While Indonesia extends over 17,000 islands, only Java and Sumatra have railways, but there are plans for Sulawesi and Kalimantan. The first railway of 25 km (15½ miles), in what were then the Dutch East Indies, opened in 1867 from Semarang to Tanggung. It used 1,435 mm (4 ft 8½ in) track but railways converted to 1,067 mm (3 ft 6 in) gauge, mostly during the Japanese occupation. Much of the network, 6,062 km (3,767 miles) long, was established by Dutch colonialists (1800–1945), initially as private railways but later by the government. Buitzenzorg (Bogor) was connected to Surabaya in 1894. After Indonesian independence in 1945 and full sovereignty recognition in 1949, railways were combined and nationalized in 1958 as Indonesian State Railways. This was reorganized into a public company in 1991, and corporatized as PT Kereta Api in 1998.

Java's railway extends from Merak in the north-west, eastwards to Banyuwangi and the port of Ketapang for ferries to Bali. The two main lines are from Jakarta to Surabaya and on to Banyuwangi (page 58), and the southerly line from Jakarta to Yogyakarta and on to Surabaya (page 60). Sumatra has three unconnected rail networks – Aceh to Medan (north-east), Padang to the east in West Sumatra, and Bandar Lampung to Palembang (south).

A West Sumatran railway is part of the Ombilin Coal Mining Heritage of Sawahlunto UNESCO World Heritage Site. The region's first commercial coal mine was located in a valley along the Bukit Barisan Mountains east of Padang. The remote town was connected to Emmahaven Port (now Teluk Bayur) by a railway developed from 1889 to 1894. The mine closed in the early twenty-first century, but Ombilin Train Museum is one of two in Indonesia; the other is Ambarawa in Central Java (page 58).

Jakarta's LRT operates on standard gauge, and a railway under construction in Sulawesi runs on standard gauge. The high-speed railway from Jakarta to Bandung opened in late 2022.

LAO PDR

The Lao People's Democratic Republic (Laos) is the region's only landlocked nation, but a new line from the Chinese border through it to Thailand makes it 'land linked'. With six million citizens, Lao PDR is also one of the region's smallest and poorest nations – the railway presents opportunities to improve its fortunes but mostly benefits its neighbours. The short railway extending over the Mekong River from Nong Khai into Thanaleng (page 98) will be extended with a new track of 414 km (257 miles) extending from Boten (Lao PDR) / Mohan (China) to Thanaleng. The standard-gauge electrified track connects to the Chinese network, and to a line and bridge under construction across the Mekong. This Chinese initiative enables passengers to travel to popular Lao destinations like Vientiane Tay (Main Station), Vang Vieng and Luang Prabang. Passenger trains operate at a maximum speed of 160 km/h (100 mph).

MALAYSIA

Malaya's first railway between Taiping and Port Weld (Kuala Sepetang) was initiated by the British. Opened in 1885, it transported tin ore, but in the 1980s the line was dismantled and all that remains is the station sign. The network linked Kuala Lumpur and Klang in 1886. Taiping remains a stop on the West Coast Line (page 64) that extends from Johor (with an extension over the Johor Strait Causeway to Woodlands, Singapore), northwards to Padang Besar on the Malaysia-Thai border, where it seamlessly connects to the Thai network. The East Coast Line (page 70) extends from Gemas, a junction on the West Coast Line, through to Tumpat in Kelantan. Nicknamed the 'Jungle Railway', it offers rugged splendour and access to Taman Negara. Both lines, of 1,000 mm (3 ft 3 in) gauge, are operated by Keretapi Tanah Melayu (KTMB) and extend 1,699 km (1,055 miles), with 25 per cent double tracked and electrified. The East Coast Rail Link (ECRL) of 665 km (407 miles) from Port Klang (Kuala Lumpur) to Kota Bharu, Kelantan, is under construction.

Kuala Lumpur has a good intra-city network that includes airport lines, light rail and monorail.

The first railway on Borneo opened in 1896 to transport produce from Tenom Valley to Jesselton (Kota Kinabalu) in British North Borneo, now the Malaysian state of Sabah (page 80).

MYANMAR

The former British colony of Burma is not without problems but is a fascinating country for train exploration. Yangon (Rangoon) is its principal gateway, while destinations like Mandalay, Bagan and Inle Lake appeal to travellers. With a route distance covering 6,200 km (3,853 miles) of mostly single track, the network operated by Myanma Railways is the region's second largest. Burma's first railway of 262 km (163 miles) between Rangoon (now Yangon) and Prome opened in 1877. Known as the Irrawaddy Valley State Railway, it adopted a 1,000 mm (3 ft 3 in) gauge. An extensive expansion, then nationalization, followed. During the Japanese occupation, some tracks were removed, while the Burma-Siam Railway was built (page 100). Rebuilding began with independence

in the 1950s and while maintenance was not paramount, the network is now being rebuilt. The main line is the north ('up' trains) to south ('down' trains) line from Yangon to Mandalay, while secondary lines service Bagan and Lake Inle. The branch line from Mandalay to Pyin-Oo-Lwin (Maymyo) for Lashio is an iconic journey that crosses the legendary Gokteik Viaduct (page 90). The Myanmar network only operates domestically, but lines to Thailand, India and China are being considered.

THE PHILIPPINES

The Philippine National Railway (PNR) operates one intercity, narrow-gauge railway from Manila to Legazpi, 468 km (291 miles) to the south-east on Luzon Island. Trains depart Manila's Tutuban Station, stopping at Calama, Lucena, Naga, Polangui and Ligao en route to Legazpi. Typhoons have disrupted this *Bicol Express* service, and it is best to check whether the overnight train is operating. Carriages are ex-Japanese stock, offering air-conditioned sleepers, reclining seats and economy class. PNR also operates metro trains on Manila's North South Commuter Railway Project.

SINGAPORE

The rail network on this 714 km² (276 sq mile) island beyond the southernmost point on the Malay Peninsula is highly efficient, and used by 2.2 million commuters daily. The plan is to extend the current network of 202 km (126 miles) to 400 km (249 miles) by 2040, and to have 80 per cent of households within 10 minutes of a station. Singapore's first steam railway opened in 1877 and tramways followed, as did trains originating in Malaya. Tanjong Pagar Station, built in 1932, was once the terminus for trains arriving from Malaysia, but the last train operated in 2011. Singapore's Mass Rapid Transit (MRT) was established in 1987 to develop an intra-island network. It is underground in the city and elevated in other parts. Trains are serviced in the world's largest underground depot. There are currently six MRT lines of 1,435 mm (4 ft 8 in) gauge using mostly driverless cars in six-carriage sets. A Rapid Transit System (RTS) is planned to cross the causeway to Bukit Changar in Johor. The *Eastern & Oriental Express* (page 74) departs from Singapore's Woodlands Station. There is a monorail to Sentosa Island.

THAILAND

The first railway to operate in what was then the Kingdom of Siam opened in 1894 between Bangkok and Samut Prakan. By 1895 the first service on the Northern Line from Bangkok to Ayutthaya of 71 km (44 miles) began, and the first section of 150 km (93 miles) on the Southern Line from Thonburi (Bangkok) to Phetchaburi opened in 1903. Not all lines opened as 1,000 mm (3 ft 3 in) gauge, but they became standardized and continue to today. Some 4,346 km (2,700 miles) is laid mostly as single track, except on the busiest sections, but very little is electrified. Agreements have been signed with China to enable expansion of the Thai network and for Chinese goods to access global markets.

There are several daily trains to most destinations, including overnight sleepers to Chiang Mai, Hat Yai, Nong Khai and Ubon Ratchathani. Passengers can travel in first, second or third class, with sleepers in the first two classes. First-class, air-conditioned carriages have private compartments with upper and lower bunk beds, second class carriages have air-conditioning with upper and lower bunk bedding along each carriage, and second-class, fan-cooled berths have a similar arrangement. Meals are available on longer journeys, and some trains have a restaurant car.

There are five main rail routes, with some connecting to Malaysia, Lao PDR and the Cambodian border. These routes are the Southern Line (Bangkok to Malaysia), Northern Line (Bangkok to Chiang Mai), North-eastern Line (Bangkok to Lao PDR and Ubon Ratchathani), Kanchanaburi (Bangkok to Nam Tok) and Eastern Line (Pattaya and the Cambodian border).

A fascinating train operates from Bangkok to Mae Klong on the Gulf of Thailand. In sections, it passes through markets that are disassembled as trains pass. This line, 67 km (42 miles) long, from Wongwian Yai to Samut Songkhram, is Thailand's slowest train. It is unusual in that the market is located across the line. It is known to the locals as 'umbrella pull-down market' because trading is disrupted as trains pass.

Trains are operated by the State Railway of Thailand, while the privately operated *Eastern & Oriental Express* (page 74) is hauled by a State Railway locomotive through Thailand.

VIETNAM

The first train lines and tramlines developed in what was then part of French Indochina were established in the 1880s by French colonialists. Vietnam's principal line connects the two cities of Ho Chi Minh City (Saigon) in the south with the capital Hanoi in the north. Work on the line took 30 years and was completed in 1936. Afterwards, the golden years of rail travel featured luxurious carriages, but services were disrupted during the Second World War and the Vietnam War. Railways were quickly restored as a national priority when Vietnam was unified in 1975. State-owned Vietnam Railway operates a 2,600 km (1,600 mile) metre-gauge railway.

International trains operate into China, and lines are being considered between Vietnam and Cambodia plus Lao PDR. A high-speed train has been proposed between Vietnam's two principal cities.

There are more than 60 million motorbikes in Vietnam and its main cities are highly congested, but metro systems under construction should help alleviate problems. Hanoi's first metro of more than 12.4 km (7.7 miles), with 12 stations, extends from Nhon to Hanoi Railway Station. The capital has plans for nine metro lines and three monorails by 2050. Work is also progressing on the Ho Chi Minh City metro.

Opposite A Myanma Railways train operating on the line near the famous Gokteik Viaduct in north-east Myanmar.

CAMBODIA
PHNOM PENH TO SIHANOUKVILLE

CAPITAL TO THE COAST

The southern line to the port and the beaches between Sihanoukville and Kampot covers a distance of 254 km (158 miles). While most tourists visiting Cambodia are attracted to the Angkor civilization around Siem Reap, others travel to relax on Cambodia's beaches.

Phnom Penh, dating back to 1432, was abandoned for centuries and reinstated as the capital in 1866. During the French era, it was considered to be Indochina's finest French-built city. There are several impressive buildings from this era and travellers seeking grand accommodation should check into Hotel Le Royal, the sister property to the equally refined Grand du Angkor Hotel in Siem Reap. Both are managed by Raffles. Le Royal's Elephant Bar, with its rattan chairs, ceiling fans and period decorations, is a venue to reflect on the past while sipping a 'Femme Fatale' cocktail, created in 1967 when Jackie Kennedy visited.

With a population of 15 million people, of which two million live in the capital, Cambodia is rebuilding after years of civil unrest. Before travelling southwards, visitors can discover attractions like the Royal Palace, Silver Pagoda and National Museum, and reflect at the sites associated with the Khmer Rouge genocide.

The Tonle Sap River flows from Tonle Sap, the region's largest inland lake, to join the Mekong River near Phnom Penh. The Mekong then meanders through Vietnam to the Mekong Delta south of Ho Chi Minh City, before splitting into several branches that flow into the South China Sea. There is no train line through Cambodia and into Vietnam yet, but should this eventuate, uninterrupted rail travel from Singapore to northern Europe via countries like Cambodia will be possible.

TRACK NOTES

Two different types of train operate this route. Both first- and second-class train carriages are hauled by a diesel locomotive, and a car/motorbike transporter carriage is often attached. Single diesel railcars built in Mexico by Ferrovías del Bajío also operate. These DMU AS 1000 series ('AS' refers to 'Airport Service', as the cars were initially commissioned to service the airport) have a central door with steps into the carriage. Facilities include digital screen displays, luggage bins, comfortable seating and space for wheelchair passengers. Hawkers offer food and beverages to travellers at stops along the way.

WELCOME ABOARD

While much of the Cambodian coastline, which is 450 km (280 mile) long, is undeveloped, Sihanoukville (Kampong Som) has been discovered by foreigners. The town only dates back to the 1960s, with many new developments, especially casinos, catering mostly to Chinese tourists.

Passengers join the train in Phnom Penh at the Art Deco Royal Railway Station built in 1932. It was originally erected to serve passengers travelling north to Battambang. The line divides just beyond Pochentong International Airport, with one line heading to Battambang and the other southwards to Sihanoukville.

The scenery is mostly agricultural land devoted to growing rice. Some 85 per cent of Cambodians live in rural areas, with half its workforce being farmers. Many are subsistence farmers with some living below the poverty line.

Four and a half hours into the journey, the train arrives in Kampot, 100 km (62 miles) east of Sihanoukville. This once sleepy

Below Built in 1932, the railway station in Phnom Penh is a fine example of Art Deco architecture.

riverfront town, with its charming French colonial and Chinese shop-house architecture, has captured the attention of developers who are planning to build Cambodia's tallest building. Kampot River flows from Preah Monivong National Park, and there are boutique hotels and guesthouses situated along the riverbanks. Kampot is famous for its pepper and salt, and has inviting cafes and restaurants.

Travellers seeking a seaside resort with limited development can also alight in Kampot and travel overland to Kep, a beachside town located 25 km (15.5 miles) south-east of Kampot. It was once popular with the French and Khmer elites, but is best known today for its crab market and beach club. While there are several beaches around Kep, the best are located offshore on Koh Tonsay (Rabbit Island), and the Vietnamese resort island of Phu Quoc is close by.

Located 160 km (100 miles) south-west of Phnom Penh, Sihanoukville's port and railway are important for freight. The train's terminus station is several kilometres north of the town and its beaches of Sokha, Serendipity and Occheuteal. Recent development has created a hotchpotch of towering resorts, casinos and apartment blocks geared to foreigners. Occheuteal is the most popular for its sandy stretches, sunset views and hawker stalls. There have been efforts to clean up the pollution caused by the construction boom, but those seeking more tranquil surroundings prefer Kampot, Kep, or islands like Koh Kong and Koh Rong Sanloem.

ATTENTION TO DETAIL

The train journey from Phnom Penh to Sihanoukville takes more than six hours. Buses do the same journey in just over four hours but the scenery from the train's panoramic windows is more impressive and train life is always more interesting and interactive. Passenger comfort in most carriages is basic, although one or two air-conditioned carriages make the journey much more comfortable. Ticket prices are the same for both air-conditioned and non-air conditioned carriages and seat numbers are allocated to each passenger.

Cambodia's climate has a cooler season that extends from November to February; March to May is the hot season and June to October the wet season.

INDONESIA
SURABAYA & BEYOND

RAILWAY TO THE ISLAND OF THE GODS

Above A Ranggajati Express train offering executive and business-class travel operating on the line from Cirebon to Jember on the island of Java.

Bali and Java being islands, there are no trains between them, nor does Bali have railways. However, it is possible to travel across Java from Jakarta to Ketapang for the ferry to Bali. Travellers can explore Jakarta and visit destinations including Semerang, Surabaya and Probolinggo (Mount Bromo).

TRACK NOTES

The railway operates on 1,067 mm (3 ft 6 in) track, as do most Indonesian trains. This route crosses Java, passing possible stop-overs before reaching Surabaya (this sector is 725 km/450 miles long). The journey to Surabaya takes eleven and a half hours, with Train 114 departing Jakarta Senen Station at 4.55 p.m. and arriving at Surabaya Gubeng Station at 4.30 a.m. the following morning. However, the fastest train is *Argo Bromo Anggrek*, which departs Gambir Station and arrives at Surabaya Pasar Turi Station in eight hours. There are other day and overnight trains. Trains on to Bangil, Probolinggo, Banyuwangi and Ketapang Ferry Port depart from this station, although some arrive at Surabaya Pasar

Turi Station, 5 km (3 miles) away. This journey of 307 km (191 miles) takes seven hours.

Indonesian trains are air-conditioned, comfortable, affordable and mostly punctual. Long-distance trains have dining cars, while staff regularly push snack trolleys through the trains.

WELCOME ABOARD

While most trains depart from Jakarta's Gambir Station, train-spotters should visit Jakarta Kota, a historic station built in 1929. With a population of 11 million people, Jakarta is not the easiest city to negotiate, but attractions like Old Batavia, Sunda Kelapa, National Monument and places of worship warrant visiting.

The train passes the port of Cirebon facing the Java Sea, with Mount Cereme volcano nearby. There are some north–south lines that connect the northern Jakarta to Surabaya route to the southern Jakarta to Yogyakarta line. Cikampek and Tegal are two such stations. Semarang is another port, once important during the Dutch era and now the station for Ambarawa Train Museum, 40 km (25 miles) away.

Surabaya, the capital of East Java and Indonesia's second largest city, with three million residents, has long been a trading port. Many passengers heading on to Ketapang (Banyuwangi Baru) and Bali change trains here.

Probolinggo, two and a half hours beyond Surabaya, is the station to alight for Bromo Tengger Semeru National Park, with volcanic peaks like Mounts Bromo (2,329 m/7,641 ft) and Semeru (3,676 m/12,060 ft). Located 36 km (22 miles) from Probolinggo, East Java's leading attraction includes active volcanoes.

Arguably the journey's most scenic section is between Jember and Kalibaru. The train passes undulating countryside, where passengers can admire rice fields and distant Mount Argopuro. At 3,088 m (10,131 ft), this dormant volcano provides a constant backdrop. The train stops in Kalisat to check the brakes needed to negotiate the mountains beyond this former junction with an abandoned branch line to Situbondo. This line was originally a main line, before becoming a secondary one as the line to Banyuwangi became busier.

Beyond Kalisat, the train starts negotiating curves and gradients at the foot of Mount Raung. At 3,332 m (10,932 ft), the volcano is one of Indonesia's most active, last erupting in 2021. The track below Mount Raung is equally scenic, with hills, tunnels and viaducts at Mrawan. It also passes plantations at Gumitir, where some of the world's finest coffee is produced at estates like Glenmore.

JAVA STEAM & SUGAR TRAINS

Central and East Java has numerous sugar plantations, where narrow-gauge trains transport cane to mills. Some 30 lines operated a decade ago, but times are changing and now only one mill uses fireless trains. Steam locomotives operate on a chartered basis at another three mills, in addition to five mills that still operate field lines. The sugar industry is also transforming and larger mills are replacing smaller ones, although towns like Madiun, Situbondo and Jember are places to head for during harvesting (July to October). Madiun is 50 km (31 miles) south of Cepu on the Jakarta to Surabaya line, and Jember is 100 km (62 miles) east of Banyuwangi. Plantations in Tasikmadu, Purwodadi, Olean, Semboro and Pagotan have operated German-built steam locomotives in the past, and are the best places to visit with guidance from experts like Bagus Widyanto of Indonesian Railway Tour. Bagus has extensive Indonesian railways knowledge and provides services to global customers.

The line terminates at Ketapang Port for round-the-clock, 45-minute duration ferries to Gilimanuk on Bali's western coast. The Balinese capital of Denpasar is three hours by bus from Gilimanuk.

ATTENTION TO DETAIL

Tickets can be purchased online 90 days before travelling (the official website is in Bahasa Indonesian and mostly accepts Indonesian credit cards), or at stations. Bookings are confirmed and travellers need to print online transactions to convert them to boarding passes at a station. The boarding pass and proof of identity are required for platform access. Classes offered include Eksekutif Luxury (flatbeds available on *Argo* trains), Eksekutif, Bisnis and Ekonomi.

It is best to avoid public holidays, and travellers with flexible itineraries should purchase Go Show (Penjualan Hari Ini) discounted tickets sold two hours before travel, although train travel is very affordable.

JAKARTA TO YOGYAKARTA

JAVA'S CULTURAL HEARTLAND

The first train from Batavia (as the Dutch East Indies capital and now Jakarta was previously known) proceeded via Buitenzorg (now Bogor) on to Sukabumi to reach Bandung in 1884. It was extended to Cilacap and Yogyakarta by 1872, then on to Surabaya. In 1906 a new and shorter northerly line via Cikampek and Purwakarta to Bandung opened. This route was 156 km (97 miles) in length, as opposed to 194 km (121 miles). The Sukabumi to Bandung route was closed in 2001 with the collapse of the Lampegan Tunnel, but reopened in 2014. The service from Sukabumi currently terminates at Cipatat, near Cianjur, as the remainder of the line to Bandung is not serviceable.

Most railways were established during the Dutch era, and this and other Indonesian lines are currently operated by PT Kereta Api Indonesia (KAI). *Kereta api* means 'fire car' and refers to the original steam locomotives. The first railway operated between Semarang and Tanggung in Central Java to standard gauge width. Opened in August 1867, it was later extended to Surakarta and Yogyakarta. The line was re-gauged to the current 1,067 mm

(3 ft 6 in) during the Japanese occupation. This journey takes eight and a half hours, commencing in Jakarta and ending in Yogyakarta, the nation's cultural heartland on the island of Java. It is an exhilarating journey as it combines the hustle and bustle that is Jakarta with many cultural experiences. There are several recommended stops on the way for those who want to explore Indonesia's most populous island. Some trains also continue on to Solo (Surakarta), one hour to the north-east, and others to Surabaya. Day trains (one departs at 9.30 a.m. and arrives at 5.10 p.m.) are best for admiring the countryside, while an overnight train (departing at 9 p.m. and arriving the next morning at 5.30 a.m.) saves on accommodation.

TRACK NOTES

There are 10 daily trains to and from Jakarta and Yogyakarta, with some continuing on to Solo. Diesel locomotives haul these trains along a 1,067 mm (3 ft 6 in) track. Steam locomotives had ceased operating by 1984, although a few are in service at Ambarawa

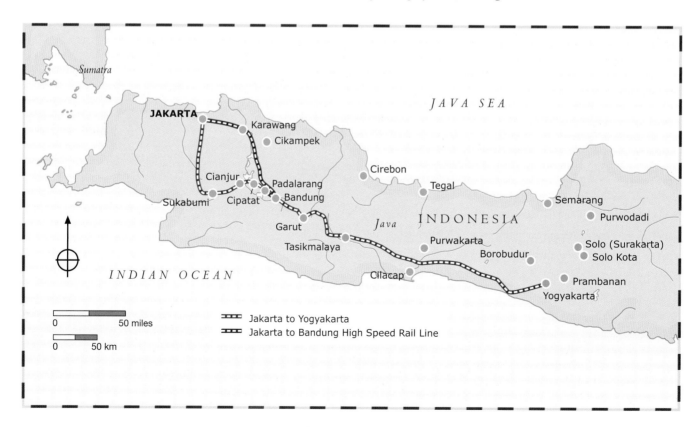

Railway Museum and sugar mills in Central and East Java (page 59).

This train has a catering car with a counter but limited seating, while snack and beverage trolleys are regularly pushed through the train. Each carriage has a toilet.

A high-speed train between Jakarta and Bandung began operating in late 2022. The contract for this line was awarded to a joint Chinese and Indonesian company called Kereta Cepat Indonesia China (KCIC). The service can operate at speeds of up to 350 km/h (217 mph), with the travelling time to Bandung reduced to 36 minutes. There are currently four stations on the route – Halim, Karawang, Padalarang and Tegulluar.

Above Steam locomotive C1912, made by Hartmann from Germany, is housed in the Taman Mini Railway Museum on the outskirts of Jakarta.

WELCOME ABOARD

Before departure, enthusiasts may want to visit Taman Mini Railway Museum Jakarta, which contains 20 steam locomotives that once worked the network. These include those manufactured by Hohenzollern, Henschel, Sharp Stewart, Kraus and Esslingen. Steam loco C1912 is housed here, with this class having been common in Central and East Java as recently as the 1970s.

Trains to Yogyakarta depart from two stations – either the main

station, Jakarta Gambir (mostly Eksekutif Class trains), or Jakarta Pasar Senen (mostly Ekonomi Class trains). Travellers interested in station design and Art Deco architecture should visit Jakarta Kota Station (formerly South Batavia), built and designed by the Dutch in 1929. It is located in the historic Kota district, which is also worth exploring. Commuter and intercity trains to Bogor, Cikarang and Tanjung Priok use this station.

Most carriages are air-conditioned and the seating varies across the carriage, but is mostly four seats, two on either side of an aisle (Eksekutif Luxury has just two seats and Ekonomi has five seats). Passengers book a seat in one of several classes, with Eksekutif Luxury being the equivalent of an airline business-class seat and available on some trains, including those from Jakarta to

Above The Jakarta to Bandung High Speed Rail Line has cut travel time over the 142-km (88-mile) distance from three hours to just 40 minutes.

Yogyakarta and Jakarta to Surabaya (page 58). Other classes include Eksekutif (individual reclining seats), Bisnis (non-reclining seats, four across) and Ekonomi (non-reclining, but newer carriages have reclining seats). Newer trains tend to be over air-conditioned and the older, slower trains are under air-conditioned, so be prepared with appropriate clothing.

While the faster trains travel via Cikampek and Purwakarta for Bandung, arguably a more interesting section is via Bogor. However, through services between Jakarta, Bogor and Bandung are not possible, although sections of the line operate services.

Bogor is located just 60 km (37 miles) south of Jakarta. It has long been a seat of power, and also a place for the former Dutch and British colonialists to holiday. While only a modest 290 m (951 ft) above sea level, average temperatures hover around 26° C (79° F), making Bogor significantly cooler than Jakarta. In 1745 the Dutch governor-general built a palace here that became the official residence for subsequent governor-generals. Sir Stamford Raffles resided here when he was the British representative in Java, and his wife is buried in the grounds of what is now the Presidential Palace.

Apart from peering into the palace grounds, Bogor's big attractions are its soothing weather and the spectacular Kebun Raya botanical gardens of 87 ha (215 acres). Initially established by the Dutch, the gardens were enhanced by British botanists from Kew Gardens. The gardens house 3,000 plant species and are arguably the region's finest. Bogor also has a bustling market and numerous factory outlets selling discounted clothing. The latter are popular with the locals, so weekends and holidays are best avoided due to traffic jams.

Those looking for an off-train deviation and more relaxed pace of life should continue eastwards to the refreshingly cool resort town near Puncak Pass at 1,500 m (4,921 ft) altitude. Puncak is located halfway between Jakarta and Bandung, and the mist-covered mountains support tea plantations and various other cool-temperature crops. The Dutch established tea plants in the eighteenth century, as the area's relatively cool weather was favourable for tea production. Return back to Bogor or drive easterly to Cianjur to rejoin the train.

Trains stop at Bandung, Indonesia's third largest city and the capital of West Java Province. Being 180 km (110 miles) from Jakarta ensures its popularity as a weekend destination, with shopping at factory outlets for branded items a popular pastime. There is an interesting assortment of Dutch colonial buildings, especially those of Art Deco or New Indies-style architecture among an ever-rising skyline.

From Bandung, travellers can take a selection of intercity trains to Yogyakarta. The most popular is the *Argo Wilis*, the premier express train service on Java's southern line. This train departs at 8 a.m. and travels through scenic mountains, with a left-hand side seat offering the best views. The scenic journey starts as the train enters Garut, with the line perched on a hill for valley views against a backdrop of volcanoes. The train crosses several high bridges that overlook fertile valleys below. It moves slowly because of numerous sharp curves and steep gradients (including the one at Cipeundeuy, where the line climbs and descends at a 2.5 per cent gradient).

Beyond Tasikmalaya and all the way to Yogyakarta, mountain views give way to scenic rural flatlands interspersed with hilly terrain and volcanoes like distant Mount Merapi.

Many trains from Jakarta terminate at Yogyakarta, although some continue on to Solo and easterly destinations. The upmarket trains use Yogyakarta Station, while the economy trains use Lempuyangan Station. The city is the historic capital of a special economic region and a centre for classical Javanese culture and arts, including textile production (batik), dance, painting, traditional music ensembles (gamelan), wayang (shadow puppetry) and silversmithing. There are some interesting buildings, including the Kraton (the inner parts of which are the Sultan's Place) and Dutch colonial structures, while Jalan Malioboro is Yogyakarta's commercial heart.

Nearby, Borobudur is a historic pyramid-shaped Buddhist site, protected as a UNESCO World Heritage Site along with the Hindu temple of Prambanan. Built 1,200 years ago, Borobudur was seemingly abandoned or partially buried under volcanic ash. A massive reconstruction was completed in 1983 and now its 10 terraces, 72-bell shaped stupas and 400 Buddha images constitute the world's largest Buddhist site. Watching the sun rise over Borobudur from behind the surrounding volcanic peaks is an essential activity.

ATTENTION TO DETAIL

While purchasing an online ticket presents some problems for non-Bahasa Indonesian speakers and foreigners (in many cases only Indonesian credit cards can be used), physically buying tickets is easy, with conditions changing for the better. Once in the country, tickets may be purchased at stations and also from touch-screen terminals installed in convenience stores like Indomaret. These machines are multipurpose and sell rail (Kereta Api) tickets as well as serving other functions. Important station codes for this journey are: Jakarta Gambir (GMR), Jakarta Pasar Senen (PSE), Bogor (BOO), Bandung (BD), Yogyakarta Tuju (YK) and Solo Kota (STA).

Seeking advice and assistance from specialist train-touring operators like Indonesian Railway Tour is highly recommended, especially for dedicated railway enthusiasts in search of the unique and unusual features of Indonesia's network.

MALAYSIA
WEST COAST LINE

ALONG THE MALAY PENINSULA

Malaysia's principal railway extends northwards from Johor Bahru to Padang Besar on the border with Thailand. From here it continues northwards to Bangkok, with the distance from Singapore to Bangkok being 1,920 km (1,233 miles).

Shuttles across the Johor Strait via the causeway terminate at Woodlands Train Checkpoint, but with connections to Singapore's MRT network. The causeway was completed in 1923, and soon after trains operated by the Federated Malaya States Railway ran the first passenger train into Tanjung Pagar, Singapore. Tanjung Pagar Station was completed in 1932 and remained Singapore's main station until 1 July 2011. The arrangement between Singapore and Malaysia was terminated then, and Malaysian trains ceased operating into Singapore. The land along the former railway reverted to Singaporean control and is now mostly a recreational rail trail.

This line forms part of the continuous track that extends from Woodlands, through Malaysia and into Thailand. While individual tickets for the three countries must be purchased separately and changes of trains are required in parts, the journey can be timed to be near continuous.

The *Eastern & Oriental Express* (page 74), with luxurious carriages hauled by a Malaysian locomotive, travels along the same line. Plans for a high-speed railway between the two countries have been scrapped.

This railway is perfect for sightseeing in destinations along the route or side trips that require off-train travelling. Depending on the time available, the recommended stops are Kuala Lumpur, Taiping, Ipoh, Kuala Kangsar and Penang. A journey of one week would provide a reasonable introduction to Malaysia.

TRACK NOTES

Steam trains once operated, but they were replaced by diesel locomotives. The line is now fully electrified all the way down the Malay Peninsula, and Electric Train Services (ETS) are used. Electrification was completed in stages, with the first section from Kuala Lumpur to Ipoh completed in 2010, and the final section, south from Gemas to Johor Bahru, completed in 2022. Passengers had to change trains in Gemas for the diesel-hauled section to Johor Bahru before its completion. The complete electrified line is from Padang Besar southwards to Johor Bahru. Electric trains can

operate at speeds of up to 160 km/h (100 mph), and are regarded by some as the world's fastest trains operating on 1,000 mm (3 ft 3 in) gauge. Sleeper carriages were previously available on sections of this line (Kuala Lumpur to Butterworth, Kuala Lumpur to Padang Besar, and Kuala Lumpur to Singapore), but electric trains have removed this necessity.

WELCOME ABOARD

Northwards journeys commence in Johor Bahru Sentral, although there are regular connecting KTM Intercity Shuttle Tebrau trains to Singapore. There are plans for another Rapid Transit System between Singapore and Johor Bahru, involving the new Bukit Chagar Station with customs, immigration and quarantine facilities.

Johor Bahru, the Johor capital, has always been a bustling market strategically located on the southern tip of the Malay Peninsula facing Singapore. It is popular with some Singaporeans who travel here to shop. Some tourists choose to stay here and cross into Singapore to sightsee while enjoying Malaysia's cheaper accommodation and food prices.

The train departs Johor Bahru Sentral and heads north to Segamat, Kluang and Kulai, before reaching Gemas in the state of Negeri Sembilan. Here, the East Coast Line (page 70) branches off the main line.

The old Portuguese/Dutch/English port of Melaka (Malacca) is a popular tourist attraction but is no longer accessible by train. The nearest station is Sungai Sebang/Tampin, 38 km (24 miles) away but accessible by bus or taxi. The line from Tampin to Melaka was removed by the Japanese during the Second World War and the rails were used on Thailand's Death Railway (page 100). There is much to see in the historic port, and travellers contemplating a visit would be wise to overnight there.

Further north, the train terminates in Kuala Lumpur Sentral, with a change of train for journeys northwards. The Malaysian capital has numerous sights that require several days to admire. These include the National Mosque, Islamic Arts Museum, Twin Towers, National Museum, Chinatown and old railway station.

The line north from Kuala Lumpur passes Rawang, Tapah Road (for the Cameron Highlands), Gopeng, Batu Gajah, Ipoh, Kuala Kangsar, Taiping, Bukit Mertajam (for Butterworth and Penang Island), Kangar (for Langkawi Island) and Arau, before reaching Padang Besar.

Those interested in exploring the historic Cameron Highlands hill station should alight at Tapah Road. The circuitous but scenic

Below Passengers alighting from a Malaysian KTM Electric Multiple Unit (EMU) train at a northern Malaysian railway station.

journey of 67 km (42 miles) is not made easily, requiring the hiring of a taxi for the steep ascent. Tea plantations, mountain trails, strawberry farms and old mock-Tudor housing create a charming setting but the highlands are best avoided during holiday periods as traffic jams on the narrow roads create big delays.

At Sungai Kerawai near Teluk Intan (on an old railway line from Tapah Road) there is a memorial to a wild elephant that died after charging at and derailing a train to protect its herd. This 1894 incident is commemorated with a sign remembering the noble beast.

Ipoh, the Perak capital, has a grand railway station similar in style to that in Kuala Lumpur. Wealth came to Ipoh and the Kinta Valley with the discovery of tin in the mid-nineteenth century. Opened in 1917, the station was so grand that it was called the 'Taj Mahal'. Like its counterpart in Kuala Lumpur, it has a hotel.

Ipoh Station is ideally located for those seeking a half-day walking tour of the historic city centre. Visit Concubine Lane,

Opposite top The train line on peninsular Malaysia is double-tracked and electrified from Johor Bahru in the south on the maritime border with Singapore all the way north to Padang Besar on the Thai border.

Opposite below Ipoh Railway Station was built in a Western Classical architectural style but with modifications such as shaded verandahs to minimize the tropical heat.

KUALA LUMPUR

Trains stop at Kuala Lumpur's Sentral, a train hub for inner-city trains, monorail and airport express. The nation's capital extends though the Klang Valley and the current intra-city rail network is expanding.

There are three LRT networks – Kelana Jaya Line, Ampang Line and Sri Petaling Line. The Kelana Jaya Line, extending over 46 km (29 miles), is a driverless system. The MRT Line of 51 km (32 miles) includes 35 stations and extends from Sungai Buloh to Kajang. The Monorail of 11 stations extends from Kuala Lumpur Sentral through the city to Titiwangsa. There is a rail service to the secondary domestic and regional Skypark Airport in Subang, while the privately owned KLIA

Ekspres Rail Link operates a 57-km (35-mile), 28-minute Aerotrain service from Kuala Lumpur to the two adjoining principal airport terminals (KLIA1 and KLIA2) in Sepang.

Since 2001, Sentral has been the main hub for trains on the West Coast Line. The original railway station is now just a stop for commuter trains, but is well worth visiting to take in what was once a grand station completed in 1910 in Neo-Moorish or Mughal architectural style. It and the Railway Administration Building opposite are impressive buildings that would be enhanced with some care and attention. Close by, the historic section of the Majestic Hotel is a fine example of heritage restoration.

Above A diesel-electric locomotive operated by KTM on the West Coast Line arriving into the royal town of Kuala Kangsar in Perak State.

the Ipoh Club, St Michael's School and numerous heritage buildings. Ipoh has experienced a tourism resurgence, with new hotel openings and its heritage being valued as a valuable asset. Parts of the city formed backdrops to films like *Anna and the King* and *Indochine*, which were filmed here. Ipoh is also surrounded by karst topography limestone hills. Caves can be explored outside Ipoh, and scenic limestone outcrops can be admired from the train all the way into Thailand.

While Ipoh is the capital, Kuala Kangsar is the royal town and residence of the sultan. It is home to Ubudiah Mosque, one of Malaysia's most famous and picturesque mosques. The sultan's current and former residences are located here, with the latter open for tourists, while royal watchers should visit Galeri Sultan Azlan Shah.

Taiping was once the former headquarters of the British Administration of Perak. There is a scenic lake and an Allied war graveyard here. Take a side trip to the rustic Bukit Larut (Maxwell Hill) hill station, established in the 1880s as a montane retreat for

Europeans who lived here. Basic accommodation is located at the 1,036 m (3,399 ft) summit. Access was either a demanding hike or a shorter sedan chair journey. The journey of 13 km (8 miles) has 72 hairpin bends and takes 30 minutes by four-wheel drive vehicle. Nature lovers visit for hiking, birding and tranquillity.

At Bukit Mertajam, a branch line departs from the main track to Butterworth on the mainland opposite Penang Island. At the terminus, passengers alight for the short passenger ferry journey across the Straits of Malacca to George Town. Penang has a colourful history as a strategic maritime port; today, George Town (named after King George III) is protected as a UNESCO World Heritage Site. An interesting site in George Town is the original FMS Railway Building and now Customs Building. Passengers once gathered here for the ferry transfer across to Butterworth for the steam train to Kuala Lumpur.

Several days could be spent in Penang exploring historic George Town or relaxing along Batu Ferringhi's beaches. The historic Eastern and Oriental (E&O) has been the hotel of choice since the era of touring the world by steamer.

Steam trams were introduced in Penang in the 1880s to link Weld Quay with Ayer Itam. Another line to Waterfall Gardens (now Penang Botanic Gardens) provided access to a quarry where the stone to build many grand buildings was sourced. Horse-drawn trams were also used, and trolley buses were introduced in the late 1920s. There are currently no trams operating in Penang, but buses provide intra-island connectivity, and Malaysia's only funicular railway operates from Ayer Itam to Penang Hill.

Trains head from Butterworth back to Bukit Mertajam, then northwards to Alor Star (or Setar). They pass through a sea of rice fields in the states of Kedah and Perlis, known as Malaysia's rice bowl states. Passengers who want to travel to the resort island of Langkawi should alight here for the overland journey to Kuala Kedah and the island ferry. An alternative is to alight at Arau, the Perlis royal town, and travel overland to Kuala Perlis for the Langkawi ferry.

The train terminates at Padang Besar, where customs and immigration for both Malaysia and Thailand stretch along the platform. The Thai train for Hat Yai awaits those travelling into the kingdom.

ATTENTION TO DETAIL

ETS trains operating on this line have toilets (with wheelchair access), luggage storage near doors and racks above each seat, and a buffet counter serving simple meals, snacks, and hot and cold drinks. Tickets can be purchased online 30 days in advance, or at railway stations, and specific seats are allocated to each passenger. Most trains are air-conditioned, with three classes – First Class Prima, Second Class Superior and Economy Class. Holiday periods such as Hari Raya, Chinese New Year and school holidays are best avoided as trains are a popular mode of transportation for many local travellers. It is worth noting that Thai time is one hour behind Malaysian time.

There are some 12 daily trains from Butterworth (Penang) to Padang Besar (on the Thai border) between the hours of 5.20 a.m. and 9.35 p.m. The journey on ETS trains takes just under two hours. These trains stop at all of the 11 stops between Butterworth and Padang Besar including potential touring stops such as Sungai Petani, Alor Star and Arau.

There are only two daily trains from Padang Besar to Hat Yai in Thailand, and these depart at 9.55 a.m. (8.55 a.m. Thai time) and 4.40 p.m. (3.40 p.m. Thai time) for the hour-long journey. Similarly, there are two daily trains from Hat Yai to Padang Besar and these depart at 7.30 a.m. (8.30 a.m. Malaysian time) and 2.05 p.m. (3.05 p.m. Malaysian time).

PENANG HILL RAILWAY

Penang Hill is regarded as the world's first hill station (mountainous location that developed as a cool-climate retreat for Europeans working throughout Asia). At 833 m (2,732 ft), Penang Hill is cooler than the lowlands, and Europeans established a summit resort here known as the Crag Hotel and managed by the E&O Hotel. Before work began on the original funicular in 1897, visitors walked to the summit or were carried there by coolies in chairs. Work on a new funicular began in 1920 and was completed in 1923; however, passengers had to change trains halfway. Modernization in 2011 ensures that an unbroken ascent delivers passengers from the Ayer Itam base to the summit in 10 minutes.

EAST COAST LINE

JUNGLE RAILWAY

This line operated by Keratapi Tanah Melayu (KTM) branches off the main West Coast Line at Gemas in Negeri Sembilan before proceeding through the centre of the Malay Peninsula to Tumpat, near Kota Bahru in Kelantan. While foreigners may refer to the train as the 'Jungle Railway', the locals simply call it the local mail train. The principal train on this line is the *Ekspres Rakyat Timuran*, and only parts of the journey are through jungle. As both main trains mostly journey through the night, there are limited opportunities for sightseeing.

The first section of the East Coast Line from Gemas to Bahau was completed in 1910, while connections through to Tumpat were finished in 1931 with the opening of the middle section between Gua Musang and Kuala Gris. During the Second World War, the Japanese removed more than 240 km (149 miles) of the track to construct Thailand's Death Railway (page 100).

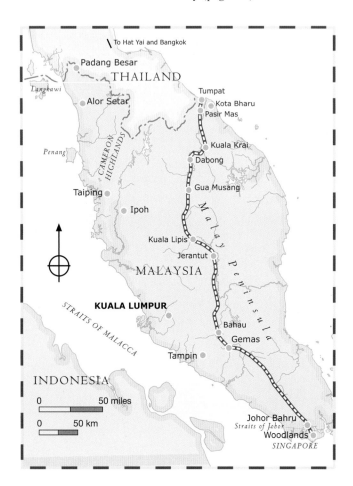

The overnight train covers the journey of 526 km (327 miles) from Gemas to the East Coast terminal at Tumpat in nine hours, so it is certainly not Asia's fastest train. However, while this train is slower than the buses that regularly service Malaysia's East Coast, the journey is much more interesting. Travellers who start the journey in the Malaysian capital of Kuala Lumpur actually go backwards to Gemas to go forwards all the way to Kota Bahru.

The planned East Coast Rail Link (ECRL), covering 600 km (373 miles), will link Port Klang beside the Straits of Malacca near Kuala Lumpur to the East Coast Economic Region covering the states of Pahang, Terengganu and Kelantan.

TRACK NOTES

The single-track line terminates in Tumpat near the Thai border. Locomotives were once relocated from one end of the train to the other via a manual turntable in the yard here. Installed in 1913, the turntable was removed in 2021 after 108 years of service to enable track upgrading. Built in England by Patent Shaft and Axletree Engineers Company Limited of Wednesbury, West Midlands, the turntable was commissioned by the Federated Malay States Railway. It was a unique turntable located at a perfect gravity point to enable two or three staff members to turn locomotives. There are plans to relocate the turntable elsewhere.

Electric-diesel locomotives operate along this route. The 25 Class locomotives (GM GT18LC-2) were manufactured by Electro-Motive Diesel in the United States, with the first arriving in Malaysia in 1991. This batch was named after Malaysian islands, while the second was named after precious stones.

WELCOME ABOARD

Trains from both Kuala Lumpur Sentral and Johor Bahru Sentral Stations are timed to arrive before the departure of ERT26 at 12.20 a.m. The connecting train from Kuala Lumpur departs at 9.40 p.m., while that from Johor Bahru departs at 7.15 p.m. The train in the reverse direction (Tumpat to Johor Bahru via Gemas) departs at 6.50 p.m., and arrives at its destination at 12.06 p.m. the following day. Gemas has little to offer travellers, although there are restaurants and budget hotels for those who arrive before the train's departure.

Above A new, Chinese-built, four-car Diesel Multiple Unit (DMU) arriving into Gua Musang in the Malaysian state of Kelantan.

While trains arrive and depart in the early morning, Jerantut is the station for those visiting Taman Negara, Malaysia's largest national park. The train was once used by intrepid travellers to access Taman Negara, but most travellers now use minivans. However, the park is still accessible for train travellers, who can alight at Jerantut and arrange with travel agents to provide either road or road/river access to the park, which measures 4,343 km² (1,677 sq miles). Several days in the park should be allocated for activities like trekking, boating, a rainforest canopy walk, animal sightings and relaxing in accommodation ranging from the Mutiara Taman Negara Resort to budget lodgings.

Kuala Lipis, the next town along the line, could be of interest for passengers although the train arrives in the dark at 6 a.m., but breakfast is served early in restaurants in Medan Tangga opposite the railway station. Local specialities include *pulut rendang*, *ikan patin*, *ikan bakar* and *hakka mee* spiced with *sambal hitam*.

Kuala Lipis, the former Pahang capital, has several interesting colonial buildings and is the gateway to Kenong Rimba wilderness. Adventurous travellers can arrange with travel agents to camp in the rainforest, explore limestone caves or kayak on the Kenong River.

Passengers who alight here could spend a few days in and around Kuala Lipis, then join the local train that continues northwards at 1.40 p.m. Another option for intrepid travellers is to alight from the local afternoon train at Merapoh Station near the western border of Taman Negara, where well-equipped climbers can attempt the multi-day ascent of Mount Tahan, at 2,187 m (7,175 ft) Peninsular Malaysia's highest peak. Access to the park is via Sungai Relau, and guides can be engaged in Merapoh.

THE LOCAL TRAIN

Local day trains on sections of this line are highly recommended for those seeking to admire the scenery and meet the locals. To do this, travellers will have to use the early-morning train from Tumpat to Kuala Lipis, or the afternoon train in the reverse direction.

These local trains are timed for children and teachers to travel to and from school. Students use the train to access Dabong for their schooling, often getting on or off at simple shelters beside the track.

Malaysian schools begin early, so the train (SH51) from Tumpat departs at 4.05 a.m. and arrives in Dabong at 7.20 a.m. It continues on to Gua Musang and Kuala Lipis, arriving in the latter at 12.40 p.m. The return train (SH58) departs Kuala Lipis at 1.40 p.m., passes through Gua Musang at 3.56 p.m. and Dabong at 6.05 p.m., and arrives in Tumpat at 9.31 p.m. The train is also used by villagers seeking services in the larger towns or transporting produce to market. Modern new Chinese-built trains now operate this service.

Gua Musang is a service town and railway stop in southern Kelantan state. It provides remote access to the Kelantan side of Taman Negara (the park extends over the states of Kelantan, Pahang and Terengganu). Near-vertical limestone cliffs (karst topography) can be admired from the station. Gua Musang is also a marketplace where locals sell their produce. The section of railway from Kuala Lipis to Kuala Krai beyond Gua Musang is considered the most picturesque, so the morning train from Tumpat or the afternoon train from Kuala Lipis is perfect, with the latter being the best timed.

While the train terminates in Tumpat, Wakaf Bharu is the closest station to Kota Bharu. It is worth noting that life in this part of Malaysia is more conservative than in most other parts, and travellers will endear themselves to the locals by respecting their customs. Tourist attractions include the Pasar Siti Khadijah market, beaches, museum, a craft village and a night market. Local crafts include batik textiles, *wau* (kites) and spinning tops.

The border crossing into Thailand is nearby at Sungai Golok. It is best for passengers to alight at Pasir Mas Station, then travel overland to Rantau Panjang on the Malaysian side of the border. The Thai train station is situated just beyond immigration and customs.

ATTENTION TO DETAIL

The train has comfortable seating and the carriages are air-conditioned, with toilets in each carriage. Passengers can chose from three classes on the overnight service – superior, premium and superior night. Superior class seating has two seats on either side of a central aisle, premium class is three across (single seat and two adjoining seats), and superior sleeper has two sleeping berths (upper and lower) on either side of the aisle. In the latter, the two seats that face each other are converted to a berth by pulling down a concealed upper bunk, and the lower seats are then converted to a bed. Sheets and pillow are provided and a privacy curtain is in place in the open-plan carriages. Sleeper cars offer 40 berths; 20 up and 20 down.

Tickets can be purchased online or at railway stations. Advance bookings are recommended and holidays are best avoided as many Malaysians use the train during extended breaks.

Overnight trains on the Gemas to Tumpat section are hauled by diesel locomotives and there are no plans to electrify the line. The planned ECRL through East Coast states could result in track upgrading on the current East Coast Line being limited – the current line could be destined to simply serve the needs of communities along the railway.

Above Rail bridges along the route are perched high above rivers, which can rise quite dramatically after prolonged monsoonal downpours.

Opposite A KTM train departing Kuala Lipis while railway staff stop vehicular traffic at a rail crossing in the town.

New four-car Diesel Multiple Units (DMUs) built by China's CRRC Zhuzhou Locomotive Co. Ltd entered service in April 2021. These KTM Class 61 train sets have a design speed of 140 km/h (87 mph), but currently travel at lower speeds. Facilities on board include comfortable seating, fold-down tables, air-conditioning, power points, wheelchair access, toilets, digital screens, audio announcements, and a small bistro serving snacks and beverages.

There are nine stations between Gua Musang and Kuala Lipis, with most being unstaffed shelters. The two-hour journey passes small villages, palm-oil estates, secondary forests and villages, and crosses the Pahang River via an iron bridge at Kampung Bukit Betong.

Adventurous travellers could just consider the Kuala Lipis to Gua Musang sector (or vice versa), including an overnight stop in either town, with sightseeing before returning to their station of departure the following day.

EASTERN & ORIENTAL EXPRESS

RELIVING A GOLDEN ERA

Steam trains were introduced into Malaya (now Malaysia) in 1885, and by 1931 the west coast of peninsular Malaysia was connected by rail from the island of Singapore in the south, to Padang Besar in the north on the border with Thailand. On the way, grand hotels like the Raffles (Singapore), Majestic Hotel (Kuala Lumpur), and Eastern and Oriental (Penang) provided the finest accommodation then and still do today. During the numerous refurbishments over the decades, all these hotels have maintained elements of their heritage and now offer refined accommodation and services to discerning train travellers.

TRACK NOTES

While public trains operated by Malaysia's Keratapi Tanah Melayu (KTM) use this line, the luxurious *Eastern & Oriental Express* offers high levels of panache recalling classic rail journeys of yesterday but with contemporary creature comforts. Since its inaugural service in 1993, the train has joined the ranks of the world's great railway journeys and is on the essential list for avid train travellers.

In the early colonial days, the train was the principal mode of transportation from Singapore northwards along the peninsula and into Thailand. While planes now make this journey in a few hours, there are many who seek comfort in the 'olden days' by slipping back into the nostalgia of colonial Malaya.

The glistening British racing green-and-cream livery of the 22-car *Eastern & Oriental Express* is hauled by a KTM diesel locomotive through Malaysia, before one from the State Railway of Thailand takes over for the journey through Thailand. In a project called 'Art in Motion', the train now includes two carriages painted by Singaporean artist Rajesh Kumar, and there are negotiations with other artists to create art on what is considered a moving canvas.

The *Eastern & Oriental Express* is very much about the journey as well as the destination. For many passengers, it does not appear to matter too much where they are heading because their immediate surroundings and the experience are paramount. The train only makes three scheduled stops on its journey – Kuala Lumpur and Kuala Kangsar in Malaysia, and Kanchanaburi on the River Kwai in Thailand.

WELCOME ABOARD

For the northbound train, well-heeled passengers assemble in Singapore on the morning of their departure. Trains once began this journey in downtown Singapore, but the Tanjong Pagar Railway Station and line has closed, with the terminus for the train now located at Woodlands Immigration Centre in Singapore's far north. Passengers now travel by coach from downtown Singapore to Woodlands.

Train staff assist with immigration formalities before the train departs and passes over the Johor Strait causeway, 1,080 m (3,543 ft) in length, into Malaysia and the modern Johor Bahru Sentral Station, where Malaysian entry formalities are completed by

Above Carriages on the *Eastern & Oriental Express* were built in Japan and originally operated on the *Silver Star*, an overnight train that ran between Auckland and Wellington in New Zealand.

passengers with the assistance of train staff.

The Pullman carriages are smartly decorated and efficient in their use of the limited space available. These carriages were built in Japan in 1972 and later operated as the *Silver Star* in New Zealand, before being purchased and remodelled for their current usage. Compared to the local trains that ply the tracks, the cabins are spacious and include the luxury of air-conditioning, toilet, shower, work table and comfortable bedding. Marquetry woodwork lines the walls, and two-tone grey carpet provides a spring underfoot.

Cabin configurations are Pullman Cabin (5.8 m² / 62 ft²), State Cabin (7.8 m² / 84 ft²) and Presidential Cabin (11.6 m² / 125 ft²). There are two berths in each cabin, and Pullman Cabins have an upper bunk that is pushed to the wall during the day, with the bottom bunk serving as a two-seater couch. In the other two configurations, day couches are converted to separate beds for sleeping.

Exclusive toiletries are provided, as is an abundance of plush towels. Brass fittings, antique lights and a decorative table give a

historic ambiance. For cabin comfort, passengers are requested to restrict their cabin luggage to just one piece and to store additional baggage in the luggage car.

Lunch and afternoon tea are served in one of the train's three dining cars, or in individual passenger cabins. Meals that would be the envy of any high-calibre restaurant located on terra firma are served during the three-day, two-night journey (Singapore to Bangkok), and four-day, three-night journey (Bangkok to Singapore). The hard-working culinary team creates gastronomic experiences at every sitting, with dishes such as *tom yam vichyssoise* with quail medallion and vegetable tagliatelle, pan-roasted sea bass served on a bed of Sichuan-styled vegetables, and coconut ice cream with *gulu Melaka sago* on the menu. House wines and beverages are complimentary, while premium vintages are chargeable. The dress code is smart casual during the day, but in the evening guests are expected to 'dress to kill' (but not in the Agatha Christie *Murder on the Orient Express* sense).

Kuala Lumpur is a brief evening stop with just enough time to get a glimpse of arguably one of the world's finest railway stations. Built in the British Raj (Mughal) architecture style, this delightfully ornate building was completed in 1911 according to British Railway specifications, including the incorporation of a sturdy roof capable of withstanding several feet of snow – a highly improbable climatic event in the tropics.

After breakfast the next morning, the train pulls into the royal town of Kuala Kangsar in the Malaysian state of Perak. The home of the state sultan situated on the Perak River features impressive royal residences, the Ubudiah Mosque dating back to 1911, the prestigious residential Malay College (the 'Eton of the East'), and the Sultan Azlan Shah Gallery. Kuala Kangsar is also home to the last of nine rubber plant seedlings introduced by English botanist H. N. Ridley in 1877. Rubber is endemic to Brazil, and

Above Pullman Cabins are converted from seating during the day to comfortable upper and lower berths in the evening.

Opposite The *Eastern & Oriental Express* travels at a leisurely pace through lush tropical vegetation.

the seedlings arrived in the town via London's Kew Gardens and Singapore Botanic Gardens. They were planted out in plantation proportions, leading to Malaya becoming the world's largest natural rubber producer.

Rice is another important crop in Malaysia, and guests on the train are taken by coach from Kuala Kangsar to nearby Kampung Labu Kabong, set among rice fields on the town's outskirts. Here they gain an insight into village life and *padi* (or paddy) production. Some 10 per cent of Malaysians are employed in agriculture, with 400,000 ha (988,420 acres) of peninsular Malaysia devoted to rice growing. Rice is a dietary staple for Malaysians, and passengers can admire fields of varying colours, depending on the rice-growing cycle, while learning about village life. Those who are sufficiently fit can join a naturalist-guided walk to a nearby hill for a panoramic view over the town.

Back on the train, the journey continues through rubber plantations and into Thailand in the late afternoon, with the open-air observation car at the rear of the train and its adjoining bar car with pianist being the preferred locations for admiring the countryside. In his 1975 book *The Great Railway Bazaar by Train Through Asia*,

Paul Theroux observed: 'and more frequently rubber estates intruded on jungle, a symmetry of scored trunks and trodden paths hemmed in by classic jungle, hanging lianas, palms like fountains, and a smothering undergrowth of noisy greenery all dripping in the rain'. While rubber estates still thrive in Malaysia and southern Thailand, increasingly more land is being planted out to oil-palm estates. In the afternoon the train passes between the two countries, with immigration and customs formalities seamlessly attended to by officials on both sides of the border.

By the morning of the third day, the northbound train has already passed through much of the isthmus of Thailand as it rattles past rice fields and villages towards Hong Pladuk Junction. Meanwhile, passengers enjoy a sumptuous breakfast served by their steward in their cabin. Along parts of the railway, houses are so close to the track that it is as if the train is passing through people's gardens.

The train continues down a spur line to Kanchanaburi, its whistle blasting away in overtime to warn those traversing the numerous unmarked crossings. Kanchanaburi on the River Kwai has a special place in the hearts and minds of many whose relatives

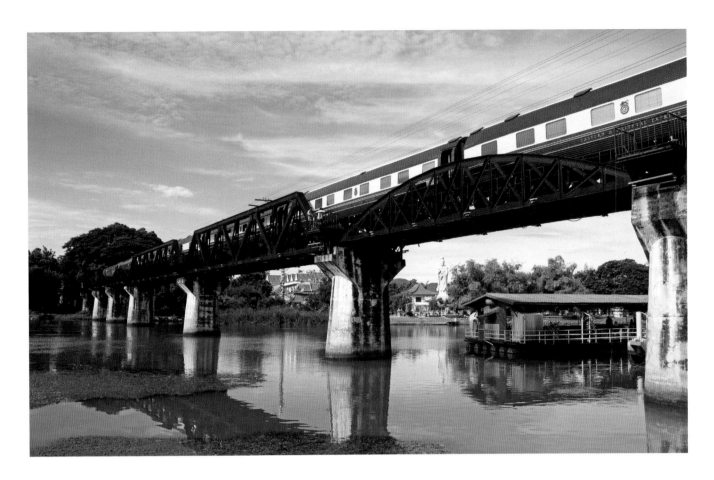

died in the construction of the infamous 'Death Railway', built for the Japanese during the Second World War. Tens of thousands of European and Asian forced labourers died in the railway's construction, making a visit to the Allied War Cemetery and Thai-Burma Railway Museum a sobering experience (page 100).

Passengers have various activity options in the town, including a visit to the museum, raft cruise on the river, or Thai cooking class. Afterwards, the train departs Kanchanaburi and arrives at Bangkok's grand Hualamphong Station in the afternoon.

In Bangkok, the Oriental Hotel on the banks of the Chao Phraya River continues the tradition of gracious Asian hospitality as it has done since 1876.

ATTENTION TO DETAIL

The *Eastern & Oriental Express* is operated by Belmond, which is responsible for other famous luxury trains throughout the world, such as the *British Pullman*, *Royal Scotsman*, *Venice Simplon-Orient-Express*, *Andean Explorer* and *Hiram Bingham*. London-based Belmond was established as a luxury travel pioneer and is now part of Moët Hennessy Louis Vuitton. The Belmond stable also

Above One of the highlights of the journey is crossing the famous bridge over the River Kwai in Kanchanaburi, Thailand.

Opposite The train travels through fertile land in Thailand where farmers tend to their rice fields.

includes luxury hotels, resorts, boats and safaris in fabled and enriching destinations.

There are several train journeys per month from Singapore to Bangkok via Malaysia and vice versa. This indulgent, multi-day journey offers guests the opportunity to sit back and be pampered with all-inclusive meals, house beverages and off-train tours, while watching the colourful countryside flash past. Different packages plus pre- and post-train journeys are offered throughout the region.

While the price for this stylish journey matches the prestigious surroundings, budget travellers could consider using the state rail systems of Malaysia and Thailand to create their own itinerary and enjoy a similar but more modest journey of discovery at a fraction of the price.

NORTH BORNEO RAILWAY

JOURNEY INTO THE HEART OF BORNEO

The loud shrill of the train whistle rings out across Tanjung Aru as the blackened steam locomotive slowly pulls out of the station on its exhilarating journey along Sabah's west coast to Papar, some 70 km (44 km) to the south of the state capital Kota Kinabalu on the island of Borneo.

Borneo comprises Sabah and Sarawak (two Malaysian states), the Sultanate of Brunei and Indonesian Kalimantan. The railway line from Tanjung Aru, inland to the small town of Tenom, is the only remaining railway line on the island, although there has been discussion about developing a railway network in neighbouring Indonesian Kalimantan, especially after the decision was recently taken to relocate the national capital to the eastern part of Kalimantan. There was once a short railway line in Kuching, Sarawak, and traces of the track can still be seen near the City Mosque. The Sabah line commenced in 1896 to become the only commercial railway on the world's third largest island.

TRACK NOTES

Two trains operate in Sabah – the public train owned by Sabah State Railway, which covers the entire distance to Tenom, and the privately owned *North Borneo Railway* (NBR), which operates tourist steam-train journeys every Wednesday and Saturday. The former is an exciting journey through the rainforest lining the Padas River, while the latter is a fun ride along a section of the same track, combining the thrill of a steam train with a nostalgic experience.

The departure of the NBR is timed at a civilized 10 a.m. so that the mostly foreign tourists have ample time to arrive from 9.30 a.m. onwards to enjoy a continental breakfast at the station before the train's departure.

The steam train is propelled along the narrow, rickety train line fuelled by locally sourced mangrove timber. There is a suggestion that it is one of a few remaining locomotives fuelled by wood.

The train's renovated carriages are opulent and indulgent, especially compared to the local train. Many travel on this tourist train for its uniqueness, while others appear to simply enjoy the fun of a bygone era. There is something appealing in the romance of steam-train travel, because it conjures up images of a nearly forgotten past, and of a relaxed and civilized mode of travel.

KOTA KINABALU
Tanjung Aru

North Borneo Railway
Kota Kinabalu to Tenom

Kinarut

Papar

Papar River

Kimanis Bay Kimanis

Bongawan

S A B A H

Beaufort Keningau

Saliwangan
Haligolat Melalap

Padas River

0   5 miles
0   10 km

Rayoh

Pangi Tenom

Opposite The *North Borneo Railway* is hauled by a Vulcan steam locomotive built by Vulcan Foundry in Newton-le-Willows in the United Kingdom.

Top The train passes a variety of landscapes including mangrove forests.

Left Locomotive 6-016 was built in 1954 and is one of the last remaining wood-burning locomotives in the world.

RAIL, ROAD & RIVERS

Adventurous travellers should consider joining a long day tour that starts before dawn with a road journey to Tenom, a train ride and white-water rafting on the Padas River, before returning to Kota Kinabalu at sunset. On arriving in Tenom by road, adventurers join the morning train and alight in the middle of nowhere. They then shoot the rapids and raft the white tops of the grade four Padas River, before joining the afternoon train back to Tenom. The exhilarating day ends with a coach journey back to the state capital. Interested adventurers should make enquiries with companies such as Amazing Borneo Tours (www.amazingborneo.com).

CHARTING NORTH BORNEO'S HISTORY

In the nineteenth century, what is now the Malaysian state of Sabah became embroiled in European expansionism. Originally part of the Sultanates of Sulu (the island of Mindanao in what is now the Philippines) and Brunei, a territorial concession was initially granted to the American Trading Company of Borneo. In 1876 this was purchased by German-born Gustav Overbeck, the then Hong Kong-based consul for the Austro-Hungarian Empire. He initiated a joint venture with Dent & Co, a large Hong Kong-based British merchant house. The entrepreneurial Dent Brothers established the North Borneo Chartered Company and took full control of establishing the British protectorate of North Borneo. The company was established in 1888 to administer and exploit the territory's resources. Its activities were curtailed during the Second World War, and in 1946 the administration was fully assumed by the Crown Colony Government. This lasted until 1963, when North Borneo became part of Malaysia and was renamed Sabah.

Known as the Sabah Dispute, the sovereignty over parts of Sabah remains an ongoing dispute between the Philippines and Malaysia with the former claiming that Eastern Sabah was never relinquished. Malaysia understands these claims to be a non-issue as it interprets an 1878 agreement between the Sultanate of Sulu and the British North Borneo Company as that of cession (the assignment of property to another entity). Malaysia also claims that Sabahans exercised their right to self-determination when they joined the Malaysian Federation in 1963.

This dispute occasionally becomes volatile with armed incursions by claimants to the throne of the Sultanate of Sulu into Eastern Sabah but far away from the *North Borneo Railway*.

The steam train is a joint venture begun in 2000 between Sutera Harbour Resort and the Sabah State Railway. It accommodates 80 passengers in five fully renovated, colonial-style carriages pulled by an 82-tonne (90-ton) Vulcan steam engine made by the Vulcan Foundry Ltd in Newton-le-Willows, Lancashire, England. It successfully recreates an era when the state was known as British North Borneo. At that time the train offered a lifeline for those who lived in this part of Sabah.

For many locals the train line all the way to Tenom operated by Sabah State Railway was once the only means to access the remote Padas Valley. The railway opened up the area for growing tobacco, then rubber, but now roads provide quicker access to the outside world for the residents of Tenom. Work on the line was initiated by William C. Cowrie, Chairman of the North Borneo Chartered Company. The train once continued further north-west from Tenom to Malalap, but this section was subsequently abandoned.

Today, the local train is recommended for 'trainspotters', who will rate this unique railway as an essential Asian train journey because it is not only cheap but also full of character and characters.

WELCOME ABOARD

Passengers can imagine the days of the British North Borneo Chartered Company and the British Colonial Office, when young Englishmen set out on their tropical adventures as planters and plantation managers in the mystical Far East. Typically, they would have been young men fresh out of school heading off into the wilds of Borneo in search of adventure and riches beyond their wildest imagination.

The NBR operates from Tanjung Aru through the township of Kinarut on its journey to Papar. Tien Shi Buddhist Temple in Kinarut is the first of several stops and, being a colourful building, most tourists enjoy the opportunity to give it a closer inspection, while the locals seem amused at the interest shown in an activity that is so everyday to them.

With a flourish of whistle blowing, the train continues and passes through mangrove swamps and rice fields, where water buffaloes graze in the *padi* fields beside the track. Rural roads cross the line and the train driver works overtime on the whistle to warn motorists.

The train crosses a steel trestle bridge over the Papar River into Papar, where it stops for 45 minutes for passengers to experience this 'rice bowl' township and the local market (called a *tamu* in this part of the world). Rice grown around the town is a dietary staple for Malaysians. While the passengers enjoy the market, the locomotive is turned on a huge turntable for the return journey.

On the way back drinks and lunch are served by a crew of enthusiastic young pith-helmeted stewards. Lunch is delivered in traditional tiffin containers as it would have been in the colonial days. This unique culinary experience highlights an exotic blend of Asian and Western treats, but with an emphasis on popular Malaysian delights. Wine and beer are offered at reasonable prices. The free flow of lemon squash is most welcome, given that the

open windows ensure that the carriage interior remains reasonably warm. Ceiling fans whirr away and maintain the authenticity of the colonial era before the concept of air-conditioning.

The carriage exteriors and interiors have been refurbished in the style of a nineteenth-century train. Each exterior is painted in the traditional forest green and cream, while brass logos feature the original design of a tiger standing on the royal crown while holding a rail wheel.

ATTENTION TO DETAIL

The NBR departs Tanjung Aru Station every Wednesday and Saturday at 10 a.m. and arrives back at 1.40 p.m. The price is all inclusive of transport, meals and some beverages, while guests staying at Sutera Harbour also enjoy complimentary transfers to and from the resort. Bookings are recommended, and tickets can be purchased online via Sutera Harbour or travel agents.

The public train can take up to six hours to reach its destination and delays are not uncommon. The journey by rail of 140 km

Above Some of the stations along the Padas Valley beyond Beaufort are nothing more than a protective shelter in the middle of the rainforest.

Opposite The service from Tenom to Halogilat is operated by a two-carriage railcar.

(87 miles) is considered the ultimate one to Tenom, embracing spending the night there (there is an excellent agricultural research station nearby with a comprehensive display of tropical plants), then catching the train back to civilization the next morning. Tickets can be purchased at any station on the network. Coffee is grown in Tenom, and sampling the local brew is an essential activity while in the town.

MYANMAR
YANGON'S CIRCLE LINE

LIFE IN THE SLOW LANE

This journey around Myanmar's (formerly Burma) largest city of Yangon (formerly Rangoon) on the Yangon River is insightful in offering a window into the lives led by many of the city's 7.5 million residents. In recent years Myanmar has been in the news for mostly the wrong reasons. Travellers to Myanmar need to be mindful of the ever-changing political situation, but those who travel here will be rewarded with fascinating scenery, enchanting culture, hallmark heritage sites and people who appreciate tourists.

While the nation's modern capital is Naypyidaw, it was Yangon up until 2006. Yangon remains the most populous city, with many residents dependent on the train. Travellers are welcome to share a journey with others who use the trains to access work, schools,

universities and homes, as well as those transporting their produce to and from markets. Many markets are staged in the open air and often beside the railway. Market nodes develop all over Myanmar where people get on or alight from their mode of transportation, so many railway stations on Yangon's Circle Line are quasi markets.

Travellers assert that this journey provides an opportunity to appreciate the essence of Yangon; an existence endured on a daily basis. Myanmar is one of the region's poorest countries, and trains are one of a few means for most to travel economically.

TRACK NOTES

This double-track loop line was opened by the British in 1954. It is 46 km (28.5 miles) long, and trains on the full circuit stop at 39 stations. The route and stations through suburban, semi-rural and satellite townships are detailed on ticket-office maps.

Both old and new rolling stock is operated by Myanma Railways, with the newer, ex-Japan Railway (some trains still have the distinctive 'JR' on them), six-car diesel sets making the loop much faster than the older diesel locomotive-hauled trains (110 minutes rather than three hours). Funds provided by Japan International Cooperation Agency (JICA) were used for track and signalling upgrades to enable these new trains to ply the rails.

WELCOME ABOARD

Most passengers join the train at Yangon Central Railway Station, and make their choice of direction probably based on the next departing train. From Central, the line north to Mandalay (page 88) departs in an anti-clockwise direction towards Pazundaung and Mahlwagon Stations, which are also on the Circle Line. From Mahlwagon, the Circle Line branches off to the north-west as far north as Danyingon, where it turns southwards for the return journey to Central. Trains heading clockwise depart Central and proceed westwards towards Pagoda Road. Similarly, these trains head as far as Danyingon, before veering eastwards and then south back towards Central.

ATTENTION TO DETAIL

This is one of the region's cheapest train journeys, with tickets priced as low as 200 kyats (the local currency, equivalent to $US

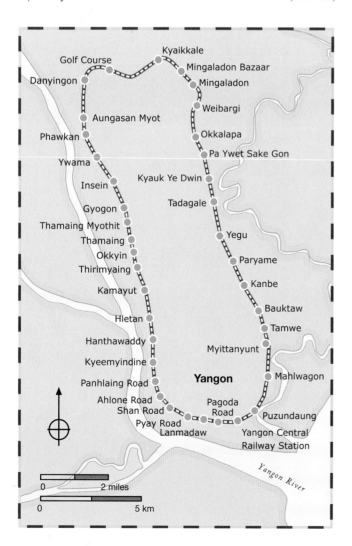

15 cents). Staff usually notice foreigners at the station, located on Kun Chan Road close to the downtown area, and direct them to the ticket office on platform seven. The best access to the station is from its southern side and Pansodan Bridge. Myanma Railways has no online presence, so handwritten paper tickets are issued by the helpful staff.

There are some 15 daily trains in each direction, with the first departure being before dawn and the last full-circle train departing at dusk. Departures are approximately every 30 minutes during daylight hours.

While facilities on the train are basic, with open windows, hard seats and temperamental ceiling fans, the railway is as close as Yangon comes to a 'metro' system. For those seeking an unforgettable encounter with daily Yangon life, this is an essential Asian journey. Intrepid travellers will enjoy the continual procession of hawkers passing through the carriages selling snacks and beverages.

It is worth noting that Myanmar is a densely populated, developing country, and that a Western nicety like queuing is rarely followed by the locals. Travellers are advised to relax, enjoy the experience and go along for the ride. You can alight from the train in areas that look interesting and walk to the next station, as the distances are not great.

The Circle Line is a functional commuter system serving important local needs. The fact that tourists view this as a window on daily life is mostly lost on the locals, who have little choice but to use the train. Travellers need to appreciate that while the journey is authentic, it can be hot, crowded, bumpy and slow. However, they can always alight from the train, visit a market, cross to the other platform and take the next train or a taxi back to Central.

YANGON TO MANDALAY & BEYOND

MAIN NORTH LINE

Rudyard Kipling wrote about 'the road to Mandalay', whereas those who now take the train will refer to their journey as 'the railway to Mandalay'. This journey commences in Yangon (formerly Rangoon) and proceeds north to Mandalay via Naypyidaw, the capital.

Despite Kipling visiting Burma for just three days on his journey from Calcutta to San Francisco, Rangoon left a lasting impression on the young English writer. His 1892 poem 'Mandalay' evoked a sense of enchantment with the exotic East and sowed seeds of wanderlust for many adventurers.

The railway connects the nation's central railway stations of Yangon and Mandalay. The first connection between the two was made in 1889, when the line was extended from Taungoo to Mandalay. Taungoo marks the border with Upper Burma and is the halfway point for the main North Line. This and other lines were introduced when Burma was a British colony, but they were neglected and poorly maintained. The situation is changing as this line and other infrastructure are being rebuilt with Chinese and Japanese assistance. Adventurous travellers can use the line to Mandalay to access other destinations, like Bago, Naypyidaw and Thazi (Lake Inle).

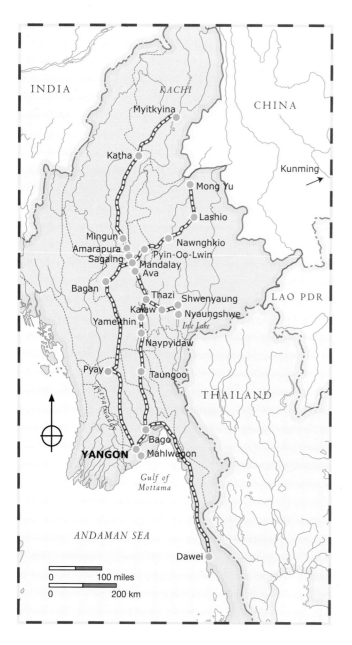

TRACK NOTES

The line from Yangon to Mandalay is 620 km (287 mile) long, and is serviced by three daily trains. The 'up' train proceeds to Mandalay, while the 'down' train operates from Mandalay to Yangon.

Myanmar's rail network is mostly single track but is slowly being rebuilt and expanded, with this main line being upgraded to double track. This project is proceeding in three phases – Yangon to Taungoo (267 km/166 miles), Taungoo to Yameithin (175 km/109 miles) and Yameithin to Mandalay (178 km/111 miles). The first two phases have been completed and the third is ongoing.

WELCOME ABOARD

Most visitors arrive in Myanmar via Yangon, the main air gateway. There are currently no international railways into or out of Myanmar, but connections through to China, India and Thailand have been proposed.

The country's largest city of 5.3 million residents has numerous attractions, with the Yangon Circle Train (page 86) being an essential journey for trainspotters. Other attractions include Sule Pagoda, the 2,000-year-old Shwedagon Pagoda and Bogyoke Aung San Market. Myanmar's most revered Buddhist site, the Shwedagon Pagoda is covered in layers of gold sheathes. Monks in dusty red robes and worshippers pray alongside each other.

Above Trains of the Myanma Railways provide the opportunity for adventurous travellers to explore some remote parts of the country.

Left Enthusiastic sellers constantly pass through the train offering snacks.

The city's grand hotel, opened in 1901, is the Strand, overlooking the Yangon River. It was once under the same ownership as Singapore's Raffles and Penang's Eastern and Oriental Hotels. Now fully restored, its suites attract discerning travellers seeking refined and discrete service. Guests can relive the colonial era in its restaurant and cafe, or savour signature cocktails like 'Strand Sour' or 'Strand Sling' in Sarkies Bar.

The journey to Mandalay begins at Yangon Central, a short distance from the Strand. Other trains to catch from here include those to the UNESCO World Heritage Site of Bagan, plus Dawei (in the south), Kalaw (for Inle Lake via Thazi) and Pyay.

The North Line passes Mahlwagon on Yangon's suburban network. Afterwards, the train passes farms dominated by *padi* fields. Myanmar remains an agrarian society, with 70 per cent of the population living in rural districts where growing rice on small holdings is the main activity.

Bago (previously Pegu) is the first stop, and a destination worth exploring for those travelling at a leisurely pace. Bago also makes a suitable day trip for those staying in Yangon. The town, founded more than 1,400 years ago, is dominated by the Shwemawdaw Paya, which is 114 m (374 ft) tall and is near the station. Another temple, Shwethalyaung Paya, is home to a huge reclining Buddha, while the market is lively and Bago has good accommodation.

Naypyidaw, Myanmar's capital since 2006, is 329 km (200 miles) north of Yangon. Like many planned global capitals, it is still developing its own character and soul. There are museums, gardens and pagodas extending over a large area, but most people continue directly to Thazi or Mandalay.

Thazi is the stop for those heading to Inle Lake. Alight here for the train to Shwenyaung via Kalaw and on to the lake. This means overnighting in Thazi for the morning train. Tourism in Thazi is developing slowly, so its infrastructure is rudimentary. The slow train from Thazi should appeal to enthusiasts for the amazing scenery on the journey of 247 km (154 miles) to its Shwenyaung terminus and switchbacks once the train enters Kalaw Hills. Kalaw, a former British hill station, appeals for its cooler weather and historic Kalaw Hotel. Nyaungshwe is the most picturesque Inle Lake town.

Those heading straight to Mandalay stay on the train at Thazi and travel the remaining three hours to arrive at the seven-storey station that includes a hotel. Mandalay, or the Golden City, was the former capital before the British took control, but it retains cultural and religious significance for the nation. Attractions in Myanmar's second largest city include Mandalay Hill, Mandalay Fort, Shwenandaw Kyaung (just outside the moated palace), Kuthodaw Paya (the world's largest 'book'), Zegyo Bazaar, and sites of interest in surrounding areas, like Amarapura, Ava, Sagaing, U Bein Bridge and Mingun.

Many travellers choose to travel from Mandalay to the famous temples of Bagan, or vice versa by riverboat along the Ayeyarwady (Irrawaddy) River. The most luxurious vessel is the *Road to Mandalay*, a converted Rhine River cruiser. This epic journey is operated by luxury brand Belmond, which conducts legendary rail journeys like the *Orient Express* and *Eastern & Oriental Express* (page 74). Bagan is one of world's wondrous archaeological sites, with more than 10,000 religious monuments across 40 km² (15 sq miles) of floodplain.

Trains also operate from Mandalay to Myitkyina, a distance of 785 km (488 miles). The capital of Kachin State is the northernmost station in Myanmar's rail network.

ATTENTION TO DETAIL

Trains are operated by Myanma Railways, part of the Ministry of Rail Transportation. Currently, there is no website and there are no facilities for online payments. Tickets are priced in the local currency, kyat (pronounced chat). Ex-Japanese trains operate on most services along the line, and passengers can book ordinary and first-class seats as well as sleepers.

Ponderous, bumpy and with few frills, Myanmar rail travel offers intimate glimpses of people and places. Assistance in Myanmar is recommended, and Sampan Travel can arrange a journey on the Circular Train through Yangon's underbelly, or across the Gokteik Viaduct in Shan State. Hardier travellers may wish to travel to Katha, the setting for George Orwell`s *Burmese Days*, or to Myitkyina with its towering blue Kachin Mountains.

At just 19 years of age in the 1920s, adventurer Eric Arthur Blair joined the Imperial Police Force and headed off to Burma. He worked in the north of the country, keeping law and order for five years before abruptly resigning and returning to England. Here, he took on the name George Orwell and documented his time in the Far East in his first novel, *Burmese Days*.

After travelling from Yangon to Mandalay and beyond, modern-day train travellers may agree with Kipling's observation that 'This is Burma, and it will be quite unlike any land you know about'.

MANDALAY TO LASHIO

The line from Mandalay to Lashio via Pyin-Oo-Lwin is a great journeys for many reasons, especially the Gokteik Viaduct (or Gokhteik, Goteik or Gohteik). The train climbs slowly from Mandalay through the valley to Pyin-Oo-Lwin, five hours up the line. This former British hill station, planned by Colonel James May, was originally named Maymyo in his honour. Like other regional retreats, the cooler weather at 1,069 m (3,506 ft) appealed to Mandalay-based colonialists. British-style bungalows and temperate gardens were established to recreate a home setting sorely missed by many. Its remaining bungalows, pony stagecoaches and colonial buildings provide a charming ambiance in what is now Pyin-Oo-Lwin.

The best accounts of train travel to and beyond Pyin-Oo-Lwin are in Paul Theroux's books *The Great Train Bazaar* (1975) and *Ghost Train to the Eastern Star* (2008). The former Candacraig (now the Thiri Myaing Hotel) is where Theroux stayed on both visits, documenting on his first visit an encounter with Mr Bernard, his convivial host. The late Mr Bernard became quite the celebrity after the author's documentation. The Candacraig was built in 1904 as a chummery for single British officers of the Bombay-Burma Trading Company, but has been renovated and decorated as a luxurious English country mansion with well-planned gardens. Town attractions include the Kandawgyi Botanical Gardens (162 ha/400 acres).

The train to Lashio towards Mong Yu on the Chinese border takes 11 hours. From the border, Kunming is another 482 km (300 miles) by bus over mountainous roads. Nawnghkio in the upper Shan States is where the all-steel Gokteik Viaduct rises 102 m (335 ft) above the valley. It is Myanmar's highest bridge, and when built was the world's largest railway trestle. Located 100 km (62 miles) north-east of Mandalay, work commenced on the steel trestle in 1899 and it opened in 1900. It was built by the Pennsylvania and Maryland Bridge Construction Company (USA), shipped to Burma and erected on site. It is 689 m (2,260 ft) long and supported by 15 towers that span 12 m (39 ft), plus a double tower of 24 m (79 ft). Each tower supports desk truss and plate girder spans. Theroux crossed the viaduct in the 1970s and said about it: 'a monster of silvery geometry in all the ragged rock and jungle, its presence was bizarre'.

Opposite One of the highlights of the train journey from Pyin-Oo-Lwin to Lashio is crossing the famous Gokteik Viaduct located 100 km (62 miles) north-east of Mandalay.

THAILAND
BANGKOK TO CHIANG MAI

JOURNEY TO THAILAND'S LANNA KINGDOM

Known as the 'Rose of the North', Chiang Mai is Thailand's second biggest city, a popular tourist destination and the gateway to the adventurous north. There are several interesting attractions on the journey, and it is possible to use trains and supplementary transportation to access ancient sites, especially Ayutthaya and Sukhothai.

The northern route crosses Thailand's fertile Central Plain, drained by rivers like the Chao Phraya and tributaries including the Nan, Yom Wang and Ping, with the latter rising in the northwestern mountains and flowing through Chiang Mai. As such, it is also the nation's rice bowl.

History notes that the then King of Siam was inspired by a railway set sent to him by Queen Victoria. Work on the Northern Line to Chiang Mai commenced after a section of the North-eastern Line was completed in 1898 (page 96). The first section to Lopburi opened in 1901, but due to delays the line to Chiang Mai was not completed until 1922.

The journey to Chiang Mai also provides access to the Mekong subregion, including Myanmar and Lao PDR (Laos).

TRACK NOTES

Trains on the 751 km (467 mile) Northern Line are operated by the State Railway of Thailand on 1,000 mm (3 ft 3 in) gauge, which is mostly single track although work on double tracking is progressing. It is Thailand's second longest railway after the Southern Line, and extends southwards to the Malaysian border (1,357 km/843 miles, page 102). The line north is not electrified and diesel locomotives operate along it. A high-speed feasibility connection to Chiang Mai has been rejected as unprofitable. Shorter journeys along this line are mostly operated by Sprinter Double Multiple Units (DMUs).

WELCOME ABOARD

Express trains stop at several stations, with the key ones being Ayutthaya, Lopburi, Nakhon Sawan, Phitsanulok, Ban Dara (junction for Sawankhalok), Mae Mo, Lampang, Lamphun and Chiang Mai terminus.

The journey begins in Bang Sue, Bangkok's central rail hub. The station is located between the Chao Phraya River, and the famous Chatuchak Weekend Market offers everything from antiques, handicrafts and fresh produce, to local silk. For those who travel to shop, the journey connects two great markets – Bangkok's Chatuchak and Chiang Mai's Night Bazaar.

Bangkok is a city of 10 million residents, and city trains ensure that its main attractions are now more accessible than they were in the past. Before heading to Chiang Mai, visit sights in the 'City of Angels' like the Grand Palace, including the Emerald Buddha, take a long-tail river excursion, and visit Wat Arun and Wat Pho, the latter housing the reclining Buddha (note that the word '*wat*' stands for temple, or temple precinct). Bangkok's street food is delicious and cheap, while the Mandarin Oriental Bangkok, with its 150-year history, is the venue for refined hospitality. Patrons can relive the era of insightful writers like Somerset Maugham, Noel Coward and James Michener in the hotel's Authors' Lounge.

Opposite Bangkok's main railway station is known informally as Hualamphong but in many parts of the country it is known by its official name, Krungthep Station.

The train passes Don Mueang, where Bangkok's old airport is used by regional and budget airlines. The first stop of interest is Bang Pa-in, with its seventeenth-century royal palace.

Many people visit the former capital of Ayutthaya as a day trip (some travel by rail and others by river) from Bangkok, but it could also be a stop on this rail journey. It was the nation's capital from 1350 to 1767, and is recognized as a UNESCO World Heritage Site. The riverine port was once a great Asian power base that traded with the region, India, Portugal and the Middle East. Ayutthaya will especially appeal to those interested in ancient temples and palaces plus architecture, and a visit of two days is recommended.

At Ban Phachi Junction, to the north-east of Ayutthaya, the Northern Line branches from the North-east Line to Nong Khai and the Eastern Line to Ubon Ratchathani (page 96). The journey across the Central Plain passes through Thailand's historic heartland and 'rice bowl' floodplains.

Lopburi, 138 km (86 miles) north of Bangkok, is not a major tourist attraction, but with several Khmer-styled temples it warrants greater recognition. It dates back to the fifth century, while

Above While many trains now depart from the recently opened Bang Sue rail hub, Hualamphong Station is an essential place to visit for train aficionados.

the twelfth-century temple, Wat Phrasi Rattana Mahathat, is near the station. Wat Phra Prang Sam Yod captures attention because of its pesky monkeys and former Hindu shrines. Lopburi is at the northern end of Bangkok's rail network and is well connected to the capital.

Further north, Nakhon Sawan is situated where the Ping and Nan Rivers meet to form the Chao Phraya. This town, located 250 km (160 miles) north of Bangkok, provides access to Bueng Boraphet lotus-lined lake, popular with birdwatchers especially for migratory birds from November to March.

Travellers who choose to inspect the spectacular Historic Town of Sukhothai UNESCO site need to alight at Phitsanulok and travel overland. This expansive site encompasses Sukhothai, Si Satchanalai and Kamphaeng historical parks, founded in the mid-thirteenth century and featuring more than 80 ancient temples recognized in 1991 for their cultural significance. These historic parks represent a masterpiece of the first Siamese architectural styles (mid-thirteenth and fourteenth centuries). It is worth noting that the three sites are some distance apart. Sukhothai scholar Dawn F. Rooney commented that: 'Monuments surrounded by towering trees and manicured gardens in the inner cities, isolated temples on hilltops and a well-preserved production centre of ceramics for which Sukhothai is renowned stand as legacies of the 770-year-old kingdom, its landscape, order and artistic creativity.'

Beyond Phitsanulok, the daily train from Bangkok to Sawan Khalok heads west from Ban Dara Junction. The train passes Lampang and Lamphun before terminating in Chiang Mai. Both have historic temples and the lifestyle is more relaxed than in Chiang Mai, which is now a large, bustling city with an international airport and numerous deluxe hotels.

Lamphun, on the Kwang River, has a history dating back 1,400 years. Nearby, craft towns like Sanphathong Village and Pa Sang house artisans who work with silk, cotton, umbrellas, jewellery, lacquerware, ceramics, timber and pottery.

Chiang Mai and the north are well developed for tourism, with an extensive range of options, from indulgent spa retreats, to adventurous treks in the hinterland to observe the lifestyles of various colourful hill-tribe communities. Karen, Hmong, Yao, Akha, Lisu and Lahu communities live in the northern hills. Parts of Chiang Mai's ancient walled city are surrounded by a moat and it was once protected by four gates. There are numerous ancient Buddhist temples (*wats*), including Doi Suthep on a mountain 1,100 m (3,600 ft) above the city.

The Sunday Walking Market begins at sunset and sprawls in the open along several streets. Each evening the Night Bazaar attracts shoppers and diners, while the daily Worawot Market is where locals shop for fresh produce. Dine on delicious local treats like *khao sawy* (noodle soup), *gaeng hang lay* (curry) and *si oua* (sausage). Other locally grown produce includes coffee and strawberries.

Visit the trendy Nimmanhaemin area with its boutiques, galleries, restaurants, bars and boutique accommodation. Stylish resorts, bars and cafes are located throughout Chiang Mai and its hinterland. The surrounding forested mountains are popular for numerous adventures, from trekking to rafting, elephant camps and zip-lining, while luxurious resorts offer indulgent wellness therapies, Thai cooking classes, golf and designer lodgings.

Travellers can relive a bygone era at the riverside Anantara Chiang Mai Resort, which was once the British Consulate. The Service 1921 Restaurant and Bar provides an elegant historic setting where patrons can enjoy refined afternoon teas or regional cuisines while contemplating the historic site that once included elephant stables and a croquet lawn.

While the railway terminates in Chiang Mai, other parts of northern Thailand, like Chiang Rai, Chiang Saen and Mae Hong Son, are accessible by road or around the Mekong River in an area known as the Golden Triangle. This includes Myanmar and Lao PDR – note that visa requirements should be checked before undertaking journeys in this area. The Mekong River, at 4,200 km (2,610 miles) in length, is one of the region's last tourism frontiers.

ATTENTION TO DETAIL

Some trains to and from Chiang Mai travel through the night, so travellers seeking to admire the countryside should travel on slower day trains. Rail tickets can be purchased between 30 and 60 days in advance, depending on the distance travelled. Online booking vouchers need to be exchanged for physical tickets at stations. Trains are a popular mode of local transportation, and holiday periods like Songkran (Thai New Year in April) are best avoided. Tickets and signs are displayed in Thai and English, and navigating the rail network is effortless. A 24-hour system is adopted for ticketing (6 p.m. is 1800).

There are several daily trains to the north, with five heading through to Chiang Mai. Not all trains on this route proceed to Chiang Mai; some terminate at Phitsanulok and Den Chai. Food is available on through trains, although alcohol is no longer served. Most carriages are air-conditioned, and any that are not have ceiling fans and windows that open.

Travel in Thailand is best in the cooler months from November to February. March and April are best avoided due to the heat and humidity during the build-up to the wet season. Modern first-class, Chinese-built sleeping carriages are used on some overnight services, including those to Chiang Mai. For more details consult 'Facilities on Thai Trains' (page 99).

BANGKOK TO NONG KHAI

ISAN COUNTRY

Trains on what is known as the North-eastern Line depart from Bangkok and travel to Nong Khai on the Mekong River and the border with Lao PDR (Laos). Trains to the north-east branch off from the main Northern Line just beyond Ayutthaya. At Nakhon Ratchasima (Khorat)/Thanon Chiva this line branches north to Nong Khai, while another heads easterly to Ubon Ratchathani (near Pakse in the Lao PDR panhandle).

Railways were initially developed by the Royal State Railways of Siam, which was founded in 1890. The first railway to Ubon Ratchathani was completed in 1930, followed by Nong Khai in 1958.

North-east Thailand is also known as Isan (Isaan), and is dominated by the Khorat Plateau, mountains in the south and the Mekong River to the north and east.

Trains to the north-east provide reasonable access to several UNESCO World Heritage Sites, such as the Historic City of Ayutthaya, Dong Phayayen-Khao Yai Forest Complex and Ban Chiang Archaeological Site.

The Bangkok-Nong Khai High-speed Railway (North-eastern High-speed Rail Line) is under construction. This new railway is Thailand's first high-speed line and a constituent part of the railway from Kunming to Singapore. Its first phase, between Bangkok and Nakhon Ratchasima, is due to open in 2023, and the entire route is expected to be completed by 2030.

TRACK NOTES

The State Railway of Thailand operates four daily trains on the journey of 625 km (390 miles) from Bangkok to Nong Khai and back. These services include diesel-powered locomotives and diesel railcars. The on-board facilities vary considerably from third-class seats, to sleek first-class sleeping berths on new, Chinese-built carriages that were introduced in 2016.

WELCOME ABOARD

The train all the way through to Nong Khai stops at key stations like Don Mueang, Ayutthaya, Pak Chong, Nakhon Ratchasima, Khon Kaen and Udon Thani (Udorn).

Train travellers can access Khao Yai National Park, located 25 km (16 miles) south of Pak Chong Railway Station. While most visitors to Thailand's oldest national park drive there, the

Above The First Thai-Lao Friendship Bridge across the Mekong River near Nong Khai was funded by the Australian Government and includes a single-track rail line along with motor vehicle and pedestrian lanes.

train provides reasonable connectivity. Nakhon Ratchasima is one of Thailand's largest cities, with an extensive range of tourism facilities, including a museum, thriving silk industry, market and a range of spicy Isan dishes. The railway line branches here, with an easterly line (see below) serving towns and tourist attractions such as Phimai (Khmer archaeological sites), Buriram, Surin (elephant round-up), and Ubon Ratchathani for Pha Taem National Park, the Mekong River and Pakse in Lao PDR.

The train to Nong Khai heads to the north-east from Nakhon Ratchasima towards Khon Kaen, another potential stop for travellers, 450 km (280 miles) into the journey. With more than 100,000 people, the regional capital has a university, large hospital, vibrant market and some fascinating historic sites. Perhaps the most interesting Buddhist temple is Wat Chai Si, with its fascinating and unique frescoes, in the nearby village of Sawathi. Khon Kaen's evening walking street market is a lively affair for local clothing made from *mudmee* tie-dye cloth and an enticing selection of Isan dishes.

The next stop, Udon Thani, was, like Nakhon Ratchasima,

a strategic United States air base during the Vietnam War. Ban Chiang Archaeological Site 50 km (31 miles) east of Udon Thani is the centre of a Bronze Age civilization dating back 5,000 years. Unearthed in the 1960s, it is now a UNESCO World Heritage Site. Phu Prabat Historic Park to the west of Udon Thani is home to ancient rock paintings, while Red Lotus 'Sea' at Kumphawapi is very photogenic.

Many international travellers arriving at Nong Khai terminus invariably and wisely continue on to Lao PDR after procuring a visa to enter Thailand's northern neighbour. Obtaining a visa is best done in advance, but can be completed at the border. In 2008, Nong Khai Station was relocated south of the former structure and now a *tuk tuk*, or taxi, is required to reach downtown Nong Khai.

In 2009 rail services first crossed the Mekong River via the

First Thai-Lao Friendship Bridge, which connects Nong Khai to Lao PDR. The Australian-funded bridge was opened to vehicular traffic in 1994 for traffic heading to Vientiane, the Lao capital, 20 km (12 miles) from the bridge/border. There are two daily trains from Nong Khai across the border to Thanaleng (7.30 a.m. and 2.45 p.m.) and two return journeys (10 a.m. and 5.30 p.m.). The journey of 4 km (2.5 miles) over the bridge and the Mekong River, and into Thanaleng, takes 15 minutes, but is a rite of passage for many. The 1,000 mm (3 ft 3 in) track runs down the centre of the bridge, and vehicular traffic stops while the train crosses. The *Eastern & Oriental Express* has also operated services into the Lao PDR terminal and back.

While many visitors to Nong Khai are travelling elsewhere, there are attractions in the town, including its Tha Sadet market, riverside promenade and Sala Kaew Ku (a bizarre collection of giant Buddhism and Hinduism concrete structures).

TRAINS TO UBON RATCHATHANI

Between the ninth and thirteenth centuries, approximately half of modern Thailand came under Khmer influence, and eastern Thailand is a good place to explore the remains of this once powerful empire. Some historic Khmer sites to visit in eastern Thailand include Buriram, Phimai and Surin. The twelfth-century Phanom Rung Historical Park (pictured), 20 km (12 miles) south of Buriram, is one of Thailand's best Khmer sites. Its striking architecture features restored temples located in a remote and scenic hilltop site.

Pha Taem near Ubon Ratchathani is an imposing cliff face with well-preserved prehistoric rock paintings. In neighbouring Lao PDR, the Mekong River town of Pakse and the UNESCO World Heritage Site of Vat Phou (Wat Phu) are located in the Champasak cultural landscape. Wat Phou is 140 km (87 miles) by road beyond the Thai railway terminus at Ubon Ratchathani. The site contains the finest ancient Khmer temples outside Cambodia.

The train passes a sea of rice fields, with rice being a Thai dietary staple. Rice is rain dependent, and in mid-May rocket-firing ceremonies placate the sky god. The best ceremony is in Yasothon, located 575 km (357 miles) from Bangkok. The Boon Bong Fai Festival aims to appease the spirit world and generate a lot of fun. The winning rocket is the one that stays in the air the longest.

Six daily trains travel due east between Bangkok and Ubon Ratchathani and back to provide access to Nakhon Ratchasima, Buriram, Surin, Sisaket (Si Sa Ket) and Ubon Ratchathani, then overland into Pakse in neighbouring Lao PDR.

The most comfortable train from Bangkok is Train 23 (Special Express), departing Bangkok at 8.30 p.m. and arriving at 6.35 a.m. the next morning, while the best return train is Train 24 (Special Express) departing Ubon Ratchathani at 7 p.m. and arriving in Bangkok 5.15 a.m. the next morning.

ATTENTION TO DETAIL

There are four trains a day from Bangkok to Nong Khai – Train 75 (8.20 a.m.), Train 77 (6.35 p.m.), Train 25 (8 p.m.) and Train 133 (8.45 p.m.). The return southbound trains are Train 76 (7.45 a.m.), Train 78 (6.30 p.m.), Train 134 (6.50 p.m.) and Train 26 (7.40 p.m.). Train 75 is the fastest train to Nong Khai, taking some nine hours. The fastest train from Nong Khai to Bangkok is the morning train. Sleepers (first and second class, air-conditioned) are only available on Trains 25 (to Nong Khai) and 26 (to Bangkok). There is also a restaurant car on Trains 25 and 26, and meals and beverages are included in the ticket price.

Like for all other trains in Thailand, tickets are cheaper when purchased at train stations rather than online, but as seating/sleepers get booked quickly during popular travel periods, online bookings in advance will guarantee a seat. Travellers are advised to avoid holidays like Thai New Year, or Songkran (April), as many Thais use trains to return home for the break.

Below A railcar service operates from Nong Khai (Thailand) across the First Thai-Lao Friendship Bridge to Thanaleng (Lao PDR).

FACILITIES ON THAI TRAINS

Train facilities vary from modern air-conditioned trains with sleeper beds, to local trains with basic facilities such as ceiling fans and windows that open. Some six-seat categories are offered across the network, with the premium seat/sleeper being first-class single sleeper cabins. These feature a cabin with a seat that can be converted to a bunk, air-conditioning, fold-down table, sink, pillows and blanket. The first-class configuration is a double-seated cabin for two passengers, with a fold-down bed to create two bunk beds.

Second-class sleepers are more common, with the configuration being two seats separated by an aisle. Each row has two seats facing each other. In the evening these two seats are combined into bedding for one passenger; the second bunk is released and folded down from the wall above the window. Upper bunks are accessed via a ladder, a curtain provides privacy and they are cheaper than lower bunks.

Second-class seats in air-conditioned carriages are configured as four seats across separated by a centre aisle. There are also second-class, fan-cooled sleepers and seat-only carriages.

BANGKOK TO NAM TOK

THE DEATH RAILWAY

Building railways can lead to occasional deaths, but the northwestern line from Bangkok to Nam Tok across the bridge on the River Kwai is infamous for the thousands of Allied prisoners of war (POWs) and Asian forced labourers who died building the railway. The line between Ban Pong (Thailand) and Thanbuyuzayat (Burma, now Myanmar) was 415 km (258 miles) in length, and was part of the line linking Bangkok and Rangoon (Yangon). Work began in June 1942 to join with the link heading southwards from Burma. Japanese Imperial Forces initiated work on the Burma-Siam Railway during the Second World War. It became known as the Death Railway because 90,000 forced labourers and 16,000 POWs died in its construction.

Today, two daily trains travel from Bangkok's Thon Buri (Bangkok Noi) to Nam Tok. An overnight stay is recommended to appreciate the railway's heritage.

TRACK NOTES

What is now a tranquil setting belies the brutality and lives lost here. The line branches from the main Southern Line at Nong Pladuk Junction. Journey highlights are mostly along a stretch of 77 km (48 miles) from Kanchanaburi to Nam Tok, including the crossing of the River Kwai and the Kwai Noi Valley. Kanchanaburi is located at the confluence of the Kwai Noi and Kwai Yai Rivers near the JEATH Museum (an acronym for the nationalities that built the railway).

Afterwards, the train crosses the Tham Krasae Bridge (wooden viaduct), also known as Wampo Viaduct. This wooden trestle bridge is 300 m (984 ft) long and grips the cliff with its steep drop-off. This is the railway's most beautiful but most dangerous section, and the locomotive proceeds slowly for safety reasons. After stopping at Wampo, it continues on to Nam Tok near the river, with its temples and resorts.

WELCOME ABOARD

Thonburi Station is on the western side of the Chao Phraya River and on the opposite side to Hualamphong Station. It is not connected to Bangkok's metro network, and the best route is via Thonburi Train Station Pier and the Chao Phraya Express ferry. However, a weekend/public holiday railcar departing Hualamphong Station

is ideal for those with limited time as it visits most attractions. It departs at 6.30 a.m. and returns at 7.25 p.m., with time allocated to view and travel across the Wampo Viaduct, and to visit Nam Tok and the Kanchanaburi War Cemetary.

Accommodation is available in Nam Tok and the surrounding forests, and along the river. The old line beyond Nam Tok into Burma was removed in 1947. The disused Hellfire Pass (Konyu Cutting) is located 18 km (11 miles) north of Nam Tok on the disused railway. The Australian-sponsored Hellfire Pass Interpretation Centre provides invaluable information on the railway's history and the suffering.

Nearby, the Sir Ernest Edward 'Weary' Dunlop Peace Park in the Home Phutoey Resort at Sai Yok is a place to stay to enjoy the setting and learn about the railway. Named after the Australian POW leader and compassionate doctor, it provides a chilling reminder of the railway's construction and Dunlop's post-war acts of conciliation.

The *Eastern & Oriental Express* also visits Kanchanaburi and crosses the River Kwai for the locomotive to be repositioned (page 74).

ATTENTION TO DETAIL

The railway from Thonburi to Nam Tok is deceptive, and a minimum of two days should be allocated to see all the attractions.

There are two daily trains (7.45 a.m. and 1.35 p.m.), and two return journeys (5.20 a.m. and 12.50 p.m.). A morning train from Kanchanaburi to Nam Tok (5.57 a.m.) and an afternoon return train (3.15 p.m.) also operate. Seating is in third-class carriages cooled by ceiling fans and open windows.

Third-class, fan-cooled carriages as well as second-class, air-conditioned carriages are available on the weekend railcar, but tickets can only be purchased from a station, not online. See 'Facilities on Thai Trains' (page 99).

While some people may be uneasy about travelling on this railway, the line beyond Kanchanaburi remains a legacy to the many sacrifices made in its construction.

Below A train operated by the State Railway of Thailand crosses Tham Krasae Bridge (Wampo Viaduct) on its scenic journey beside the River Kwai.

THAILAND-BURMA RAILWAY MUSEUM AND KANCHANABURI WAR CEMETERY

The Kanchanaburi War Cemetery is a sombre memorial to thousands of Allied (British, Australian, Dutch and Indian) soldiers buried here. The Thailand-Burma Railway Museum adjacent is an interactive museum and research facility dedicated to those who died. It is a reference point for those seeking information on relatives and friends who worked on the railway. It opens daily from 9 a.m. to 4 p.m., and facilities include a shop, cafe and personalized services.

BANKGOK TO HAT YAI & THE SOUTH

DOWN THE ISTHMUS TO MALAYSIA

While not the Kingdom of Siam's first railway, the line south was an important initiative to link Penang in neighbouring Malaya and connections through to Singapore. Siam's King Rama V was a keen supporter of extending the Kingdom's rail network, and he became known as the 'father of Siam railroads'.

As envisaged, the route now proceeds southwards from Bangkok to the royal town of Hua Hin, on to Surat Thani for connections to

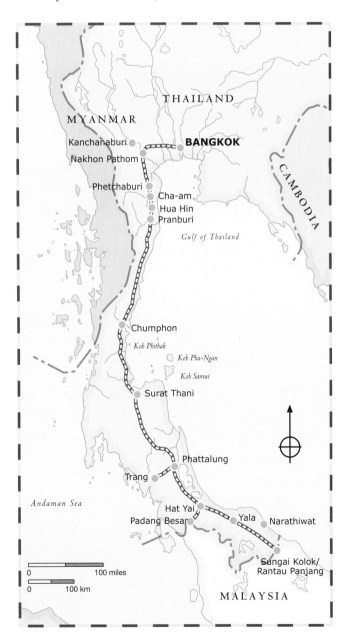

the famous island destination of Koh Samui, then down the isthmus to Thong Song Junction, 757 km (470 miles) south of Bangkok. Here the Kantang Line branches due south to Trang and Kantang, while the main Southern Line continues south-east towards Hat Yai. The railway branches in Hat Yai, with the main line proceeding further south to Padang Besar on the Thai/Malaysian border. From Hat Yai, a southeasterly line heads towards Yala, Narathiwat and Sungai Kolok/Rantau Panjang. This enables an incomplete connection with Malaysia's East Coast train (page 70), which departs from Pasir Mas on the Malaysian side of the border near Kota Bharu in Kelantan. Most train travellers entering Malaysia from Thailand use the border crossing at Padang Besar. Travellers need to be aware that Thailand is one hour behind Malaysia.

TRACK NOTES

Trains now depart from Bang Sue Grand Station in Chatuchak, north of the old Hualamphong Station. This new transportation centre, billed as the largest of its type in the region, with 26 platforms extending over four floors, is the hub for Bangkok's metro systems. This includes the new Red Line to Rangsit in northern Bangkok and an airport link, as well as long-distance trains (lines to the north, north-east, south and east). Six tracks are reserved for the future introduction of high-speed trains, which are planned to connect to Nong Khai, Hua Hin and possibly other destinations.

The journey from Bangkok to Hat Yai takes between 14 and 18 hours, with the fastest, a diesel railcar, having only second-class seating. There are five daily departures for the journey of 945 km (587 miles), with most trains leaving in the early to late afternoon, and all but the railcar offer sleeping berths and a restaurant car.

WELCOME ABOARD

Like all long-distance Thai trains, those on the Southern Line are operated by the State Railway of Thailand. Trains pass through Nakhon Pathom and Phetchaburi before arriving in the seaside resort of Hua Hin. The first train to connect with Thailand's oldest seaside resort reached here in 1911. Hua Hin and neighbouring

Opposite Thailand's most picturesque railway station is at Hua Hin where the Royal Pavilion adds a touch of colour.

Above The *Eastern & Oriental Express* and a train destined for southern Thailand at Bangkok's Hualamphong Station.

Opposite South of Hua Hin long stretches of railway line traverse secondary forest and agricultural land.

Cha-am have morphed into a continuous coastal strip of seaside hotels, resorts and associated infrastructure some 200 km (124 miles) south of Bangkok. The sleepy fishing village slowly developed as the Kingdom's first resort town. Hua Hin appealed to domestic tourists, but its development was slow up until the 1990s, when international resorts began opening along the long beachfront.

The red-and-white Royal Pavilion at Hua Hin Railway Station was used by royalty when they visited the town. Several royal palaces were built nearby as summer retreats and the seat of government for a few months every year, when official business was conducted in the town. Royal retreats such as Muruk Khatayawan Palace, built entirely from teak, are open for visitors to inspect. The royal family still maintains a retreat here.

The Railway Hotel opened in 1922 as an elegant and refined beachside resort along the Hua Hin beachfront. It was built in an era when long journeys were a luxury, and Hua Hin became an exclusive coastal retreat for Thailand's holidaying royalty and socialites. It was constructed on land owned by the State Railway of Thailand, which still owns it but leases the hotel, currently the Centara Grand Beach Resort and Villas Hua Hin, which retains

the elegance of a bygone era. Its sculptured topiary bushes are a feature, while the property also includes extensive gardens and three pools overlooking the Gulf of Thailand. Guests can enjoy elegant afternoon teas in the Museum Cafe, or play a game of chess on the giant outdoor chessboard.

The line continues southwards along a mostly single track that connected to the Malay network in 1921. Some travellers head to Surat Thani to alight and transfer to the popular resort island of Koh Samui, but there are other beachside destinations beforehand to consider.

Some destinations to explore include Khao Sam Roi Yot National Park, Pranburi and Panburi Forest Park. Further south at Chumphon, Mu Ko National Park and Koh Phithak are places of interest.

Many train travellers alight at Surat Thani for their shuttle-bus

and ferry transfers to the popular Gulf of Thailand resort islands of Koh Samui and Koh Pha-Ngan. Several daily trains also make the journey just from Bangkok to Surat Thani, but travelling times vary markedly at between nine and 15 hours. Combined train, bus and ferry tickets can be purchased.

At Thong Song Junction (Mu Ban), the line to Trang branches off to the south. It continues to its ultimate terminal at Kantang on the banks of the Trang River. Trang provides access to the islands of Koh Nhai (Hai), Koh Muk (Mook) and Koh Krandan just offshore from Pak Meng Beach, 20 km (12 miles) to the west of Trang in the Andaman Sea. The journey takes approximately 15 hours, and there are two early-evening departures from Bangkok that arrive in Trang the next morning.

Meanwhile, trains operating on the main Southern Line continue on to Phattalung and Hat Yai. Travellers wishing to explore the Thale Noi wetlands and their extensive birdlife should alight at Phattalung.

Most trains arrive in Hat Yai at a civilized time in the morning, enabling passengers to enjoy a whole day of exploration, or onward travel. The city is a popular shopping town for Malaysians who pop across the border – numerous malls, markets, hotels and restaurants in the town cater to their every need.

Two daily trains continue down the branch line to Yala, Narathiwat and Sungai Kolok for Malaysia's East Coast and the East Coast Line. These trains depart Bangkok in the early and mid-afternoon, and take approximately 22 hours to reach their destination. Few travellers venture this way because of civil unrest in the province, but those who do can enjoy sights such as Ai Yer Weng (Sea of Mist) and Bang Lang National Park, as well as beaches and places to fish. This is one of Thailand's most conservative provinces, and travellers are encouraged to respect the local customs.

The main line continues from Hat Yai through to the Thai/Malaysian border of Padang Besar in northern Malaysia. From here, trains operated by Malaysia's KTMB continue through Malaysia to the southernmost station of Johor Bahru, and across the causeway into Woodlands, Singapore.

Thai immigration and customs are at one end of Padang Besar Station, while the Malaysian facilities are at the other end to offer a seamless connection.

ATTENTION TO DETAIL

While some passengers use the train simply as a means to get from one point to another, all the trains on the southern route can be used by travellers to access many exciting seaside and island resorts, plus natural and cultural sites along the way.

Tickets for three classes of travel (first, second and third) and configurations (seat or sleeper/seat) can be purchased online or at train stations. This can be done 90 days in advance for direct journeys and 30 days in advance for travel along a section of the whole journey. Online reservations need to be exchanged for an actual ticket at a station before travelling. Book early for first class, as these sleepers are limited. Reserved seats are essential during peak holiday seasons. Most Thai trains are air-conditioned, and upper sleeping berths are cheaper than lower ones as they are slightly smaller. Train attendants make up the beds as and when required, or in the early evening. Toilets and washing facilities are available at the end of each carriage.

Trains heading north from Hat Yai all depart in the late afternoon or early evening, arriving in Bangkok from just after sunrise to mid-morning.

The *Eastern & Oriental Express* (page 74) also uses this line on its journey from Bangkok to Singapore and back.

VIETNAM
REUNIFICATION EXPRESS

SAIGON TO HANOI

The railway linking Ho Chi Minh City (HCMC, often referred to as Saigon), in the south of the Socialist Republic of Vietnam, to Hanoi (or Ha Noi) in the north, covers a distance of 1,726 km (1,072 miles). It was completed in 1936 during French colonial times, but remained intact for just 18 years. Luxurious trains operating the route were dubbed the *Transindochinoise* and took 60 hours to cover the distance. The country's north and south were politically divided during the Vietnam War (known to Vietnamese as the American War), and the line was ravaged by floods, bombing and sabotage. Vietnam was embroiled in this conflict from 1955 to 1975.

So strategic was the route that when the conflict was resolved, the new government gave priority to rebuilding the railway and Highway 1, which follows a similar route. Some 70,000 workers repaired or reconstructed 200 bridges, 500 culverts, 20 tunnels and 150 stations. When the first train from HCMC arrived in Hanoi in 1977, the reunification was witnessed by thousands of citizens waving flags and igniting firecrackers.

Train journeys begin in both Hanoi and HCMC. Vietnam is very much a tale of two cities, HCMC being Vietnam's economic powerhouse and the city that is developing more rapidly than the capital Hanoi.

TRACK NOTES

Trains operated by Vietnam Railways – often referred to as the *Reunification Express* (or Unification Express) – now take some 33 hours to complete their journey. Its name was initially given to the service in 1976 at the cessation of the war, but these days there is no one train referred to as the *Reunification Express*. Rather trains are numbered – with the best trains being SE1, SE2, SE3 and SE4. Even-numbered trains operate from south to north (HCMC to Hanoi) and odd-numbered ones from north to south.

Vietnam's railways are well developed and a popular mode of transport for both locals and increasing numbers of travellers. Independent travellers will find Vietnamese travel quite effortless. Travellers can book seats or sleeping berths (mostly four to a cabin, with the lower bunks being more accessible than the upper ones), and enjoy the journey and the ever-changing scenery through rural and coastal Vietnam. All trains on this route have a dining car selling basic but decent local meals and beverages, while

snacks/beverages are sold from carts wheeled through the train and by hawkers along train platforms. It is a fascinating journey along coastal parts of this elongated country, traversing verdant fields, scenic beaches fronting the South China Sea, and vibrant towns and cities.

Freight trains share the metre-gauge track, and freight operations often take place adjacent to passenger platforms. Freight trains

are typically hauled by a single four-axle diesel locomotive such as Romanian-built model D11H (1,100 hp) or Czech-built model D12E (1,200 hp) locomotives. In both cases a second locomotive is often added to the rear of these trains for the steep grades over Hai Van Pass between Danang and Hué. Newer, more powerful, Chinese six-axle D19E locomotives (1,950 hp) handle the express passenger trains and tackle the mountain grades without the assistance of a helper locomotive.

WELCOME ABOARD

With so much to see, the journey may take a week if sightseeing is included. Those who want to alight along the way should study timetable options in order to arrive at a destination at a respectable time.

The main destinations from south to north are Binh Thuan (for Phan Thiet and Mui Ne), Nha Trang, Danang (or Da Nang for historic Hoi An, China Beach and Lang Co), Hué and Dong Ha (for the Demilitarized Zone, or DMZ). However, there are several other stops, so sightseeing is highly recommended.

Above The railway line passes close to the East Vietnam Sea north of Danang.

Northbound passengers board the train in HCMC, Vietnam's largest metropolis, with nine million residents. Interestingly, the station is still called Ga Sai Gon to reflect its fabled past. There are sufficient attractions in HCMC to warrant a stay of several days before travelling on to Hanoi. The streets are crammed with traffic, but a Metro currently under construction will enable easier travel to admire attractions like the War Remnants Museum, Binh Tay Market, Opera House, Central Post Office, Gothic-style Notre-Dame Cathedral, and Bitexco Tower, with a skydeck on the forty-ninth floor of this 68-storey building. Several hotels became legendary during the Vietnam War or through the writings of famous authors. These include the Rex, Caravelle and Continental, with the first two having iconic rooftop bars.

On departing HCMC and three hours into the journey, the train pulls into Binh Thuan for Phan Thiet. Phan Thiet is famous for fishing and fish sauce (*nouc nam*), an essential ingredient in

Vietnamese cooking. The locals debate the nation's finest fish sauce – either that from Phan Thiet or the one from Phu Quoc Island. There are a few seaside resorts nearby at Phan Thiet and further north at the more popular Mui Ne.

There are several trains per week plus holiday trains direct from HCMC to Binh Thuan on the main line, then down the branch line to Phan Thiet, which may be suitable for those just travelling to the coast. The alternative is to alight from trains on the main line and catch a taxi for the remainder of the journey. The line continues north past Cam Ranh to its next stop, the seaside resort of Nha Trang. During the Vietnam War, Cam Ranh Bay was a strategic air and naval base for United States forces. Now Vietnam's fourth busiest airport, Cam Ranh serves regional resorts, especially those in Nha Trang.

Nha Trang, once a sleepy fishing village and home to Cham culture, has well and truly been discovered over recent decades.

After the seven and a half hour journey from HCMC, it is a stark contrast to much of the route from the south. Its towering beachside hotels and apartments offer a comprehensive range of services and facilities, including accommodation, restaurants, spas and watersports. Nha Trang is Vietnam's most commercialized resort destination now visited by local and overseas holidaymakers. Passengers who alight here can explore the fishing village along the Cai River and the archaeological remains of Po Nagar Cham

Towers, or relax on the long beachfront and several offshore islands within Hon Mun Marine Protected Area.

Those seeking a cooler mountain retreat may consider an inland road journey to the hilltop resort of Dalat (page 112). The French established Dalat as *Petit Paris* for its spring-like weather. Its lakes, forests, waterfalls, gardens, hill-tribe communities and golf appeal. Further north of Nha Trang, the central Vietnam destinations of Hoi An, Danang and Hué are popular with tourists. Those wishing to explore the small historic riverside town of Hoi An should alight at Danang. Hoi An is a protected UNESCO World Heritage Site, and it appears that little has changed for centuries in this trading port. It is similar to Malaysia's Melaka (page 65), or Galle in Sri Lanka (page 48), but much smaller in scale and more authentic than either. Terraced shops and houses line narrow streets given over to non-motorized traffic. Wandering the streets is the best way to idyll away a few days if time permits. This ancient port attracted Japanese, Portuguese, Dutch, Arab, Chinese and French mercantile trades. Its old buildings survived Vietnam's turbulent past, making it one of the world's best preserved ports. The nearby beaches of Cua Dai and the renowned China Beach are home to luxurious beachfront resorts.

Further north, the Cham Museum in Danang is worth visiting to learn more about the civilization dating back 1,200 years, when it dominated southern and central Vietnam. Ba Na Hills, a themed French attraction above Danang, is accessible via a cable car.

Both the rail and mountainous road route between Danang and Hué are highly recommended. The rail journey hugs the picturesque coastline around Lang Co, while the road crosses over the cloud-covered Hai Van Pass. If time permits, do both journeys. Motorists using the highway tunnel that opened in 2005 have the quickest but most uninteresting journey of all. The tunnel bypasses the original road over the pass. All routes emerge on the northern side of the mountain range at Lang Co, which is an emerging seaside resort.

The train from Danang arrives in Hué, the former imperial city, with its UNESCO Imperial City and Tombs of the Emperors of the Nguyen Dynasty World Heritage Site. Hué is regarded as a centre of Vietnamese culture and is the first stop for express trains after the Hai Van Pass. In Hué, the railway crosses the Perfume

Left The coast between Danang and Hué near Lang Co is one of the most scenic sections traversed by the *Reunification Express*.

River on a long, through-truss bridge. The river flows out of low, rolling hills where former Vietnamese emperors are entombed. It is possible to hire a 'dragon boat' for leisurely cruising under the railway bridge and up to the tombs. Hué was also an area of intense combat, especially during the 1968 Tet Offensive, but it has been rebuilt. Its heritage buildings in the Forbidden Purple City and Hué cuisine also appeal.

While it is sometimes hard for travellers to realize that a war was fought in Vietnam, there are many reminders. Alight at Dong Ha to visit sites along the Demilitarized Zone (DMZ) and sections of the Ho Chi Minh Trail. Many infamous battles were fought here and history hounds will want to visit the sites, using Dong Ha as their base. Some of the sites include the Provincial Museum, Truong Son Cemetery, Khe Sanh, Vinh Moc Tunnels, Hamburger Hill, Ben Hai River and sections of the Vietcong supply route called the Ho Chi Minh Trail.

From Dong Ha, express trains also stop at Dong Hoi, Vinh and Thanh Hoa before pulling into Hanoi. The Vietnamese capital and former capital of French Indochina (1887–1954) is a city on the move, as its towering skyscrapers and streets jammed with motorbikes suggest. Its wide boulevards and colonial buildings, especially in the precincts around the tranquil Hoan Kiem Lake, are places to explore, relaxing over coffee and joining the locals in recreation in sections that are closed off to weekend traffic.

Hanoi's French Quarter, with its faded colonial charm, is home to stately public buildings featuring French, local and Chinese architecture. Popular tourist sites include the Temple of Literature, Ho Chi Minh's Mausoleum, Hoan Kiem Lake, and the Old Quarter with its maze of narrow streets, each devoted to a specific craft. Others come to relax over a bowl of *pho* (noodle soup), to sip traditional filtered Vietnamese coffee at lakeside cafes, or to admire water puppetry. Those seeking colonial-style accommodation should check into the Old Wing of the grand Metropole Hanoi, or at least enjoy a cocktail at Angelina, one of Asia's upbeat and atmospheric bars.

ATTENTION TO DETAIL

Trains slowly traverse a landscape of coastal forests and farms, and on occasion are within sight of the sea. Services are frequent, with four daily departures from both the north and south (more during

busy travel periods like the Tet holiday). Two depart in the morning and two in the evening. Other trains only go part of the way, such as Hanoi–Danang, Hué–HCMC and Phan Thiet–HCMC. Despite many being labelled 'express', they are not rapid, with the fastest service averaging barely 52 km/h (32 mph). However, this is perfect for sightseeing.

HCMC Station (Ga Sai Gon) is located close to the city centre. The station was originally built in 1930 and a new section was added in 1983. Electronic gates have been installed for platform access. There are toilets, wi-fi, convenience stores and restaurants, while tickets are easily purchased from the booking office.

The HCMC Metro is being developed, with a planned seven routes extending 107 km (66 miles). Route 1 of 20 km (12 miles), with 14 stations from the popular Ben Thanh Market north-east to Suoi Tien Park, recently opened.

In Hanoi the main railway station (Ga Ha Noi) is located just west of the centrally located Hoan Kiem Lake. It was constructed in 1902, partly destroyed by bombs during the war and rebuilt in a modern style in 1976. Facilities and services are similar to those in HCMC. Through trains to Dong Dang and Nanning (China) depart from Hanoi Gia Lam Station, and to Halong Bay from Yen Vien Station, both on the opposite side of the Red River, north of the city (page 114).

The main trains are air-conditioned, with seating offered as soft seats, four-berth soft class and six-berth hard sleepers. Trains SE1 and SE2 have just a few VIP sleeper cabins that accommodate only two passengers (both lower berths). These two trains also convey privately operated tourist sleeper carriages operated by Livitrans between Hanoi, Danang and Hué. Trains SE3 and SE4 convey similar carriages operated by Violette.

Lower bunks are slightly more expensive than upper ones, and the six-berth compartments are confined, with minimal head clearance when configured as sleepers. Tickets can be purchased at stations, online or from specialized travel agents.

DALAT PLATEAU RAIL ROAD

ESCAPE TO A VIETNAMESE HILL STATION

Vietnam Railways operates 2,600 km (1,616 miles) of track, but the former branch line from the main north–south railway to the highlands of Dalat (or Da Lat) is no longer operational except for a small section on the plateau. The Crémaillère Railway (*crémaillère* is French for cog, or rack-and-pinion) once linked Thap Cham on the coast near Phan Rang with the former French hill station of Dalat in the Central Highlands. Hill stations developed throughout Asia as they offered a cooler respite for heat-weary colonialists stationed in the former French colony. Dalat's cool climate, lakes and forests ensure that it is still one of Vietnam's most serene holiday retreats. While hill-tribe people, or Montagnards, had lived in the highlands for centuries, Dalat came to the attention of the French in 1893, when Dr Alexandre Yersin, a protégé of Louis Pasteur and the first to identify the plague bacillus, identified the area as a healthy holiday retreat.

TRACK NOTES

Sections of the railway, which is 84 km (52 miles) long, opened in 1928, but by 1964 the Viet Cong had successfully blown up enough of the line to force its closure. Initially surveyed in 1898 by the French, the fully completed line did not open until 1933 due to several steep sections near the summit of the highlands at 1,500 m

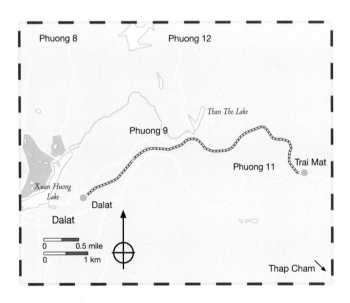

Right The clock feature of the Art Deco railway station..

Opposite A Vietnam Railways 131 Class train is displayed at Dalat Station. Built in Japan, it arrived in Vietnam from China in the 1950s but probably did not operate on the Dalat Plateau.

(4,921 ft) above sea level. Some 16 km (10 miles) of the track had to incorporate zigzag sections and cog-wheel technology designed by Swedish engineers. When the railway opened, there were two daily train services from coastal Nha Trang to Dalat and back, which included one goods carriage and three passenger carriages. The line was operated by Compagnie des Chemins de Fer de L'Indochine using locomotives built in Winterthur, Switzerland, as well as in Germany.

ATTENTION TO DETAIL

Today, the only section of the line that remains open is 8 km (5 miles) long on the Lang Biang Plateau from Dalat Station to the village of Trai Mat. Dalat's French-designed Art Deco railway station, and Vietnam's highest at 1,500 m (4,900 ft), is worth visiting to admire the large clock, architecture dating back to 1938 and old locomotives on display, including a Japanese engine that was the last commercial steam train to operate in Vietnam. There are several daily diesel-hauled departures between 7.45 a.m. and 4 p.m. for the 20-minute trip through market gardens to Trai Mat, where the Linh Phuoc Pagoda is the main attraction. Passengers have 40 minutes to explore the Dragon Pagoda and village before the train returns. On the journey, passengers can relive a bygone era in beautifully restored carriages of the Dalat Plateau Rail Road hauled by a D6H diesel locomotive.

A recent planning document lists the restoration of the entire line as a priority for Lam Dong Province but nothing has as yet materialized. While Lien Khoung International Airport is just to the south-west of Dalat, most visitors arrive by road. Who knows – perhaps one day the old Crémaillère Railway may be reinstated?

HANOI TO LAO CAI

HEAD FOR THE HILLS

The journey of 296 km (185 miles) from Hanoi to Lao Cai, near the north-west border with China, is recommended for cooler weather and adventurous activities in the former French hill station of Sapa, located 38 km (24 miles) up a road into the mountains. Colonialists found the cool air appealing and established a rail connection in 1910. This north-west line became part of the metre-wide gauge that began in coastal Haiphong and continued on to Kunming in China's Yunnan Province. Known as Les Chemins de Fer de L'Indochine (Indochina and Yunnan Railways), the railway was built in two parts: Haiphong to Lao Cai and Lao Cai to Kunming. Travelling the 311 km (193 miles) between Lao Cai and Kunming was not possible for years, but is now open on a line converted to standard gauge in 2014.

Sapa and nearby Bac Ha are popular destinations for the colourful hill-tribe communities and trekking. A cable car to Mount Fansipan, Vietnam's highest peak at 3,147 m (10,226 ft), is another attraction. Sapa is less developed than Dalat, although this does not mean that it has not been discovered by tourists. The French referred to the mountains as the Tonkinese Alps and to the locals as Montagnards (most mountain people belong to the Hmong, Red Dao, Tay or Giay communities).

Several private companies provide sleeping berths in luxurious carriages that are hooked up to the normal Vietnam Railway train.

TRACK NOTES

Trains depart from Hanoi's main station and take eight hours to reach Lao Cai. Travellers seeking to continue to Kunming need to take a taxi to the border, cross the Vietnam-China border on foot, then take a Chinese taxi to Hekou North Station for the Kunming train. Trains to Kunming take another seven hours. Many travellers require a visa to enter China from Vietnam, and tickets are usually issued only after a visa has been obtained.

Opposite Private companies attach carriages to scheduled public trains to cater to passengers who prefer luxurious overnight accommodation.

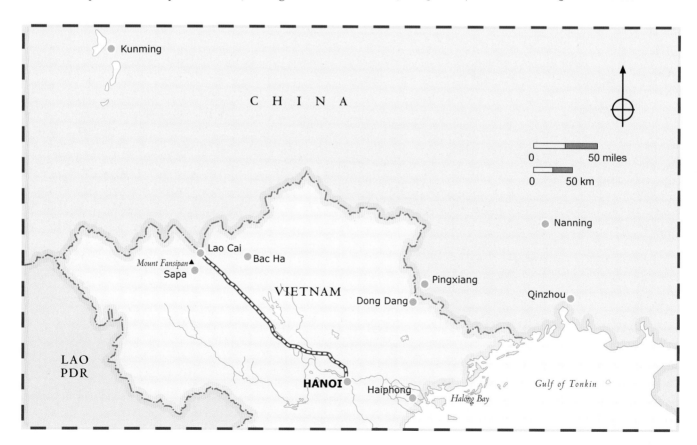

WELCOME ABOARD

Passengers can travel in hard- or soft-class seats, hard- or soft-class sleepers (hard class are three tiered, six to a compartment), and soft class (two-tier berths, four to a compartment), or in sleepers within privately owned carriages.

ATTENTION TO DETAIL

Several daily trains make the journey to and from Hanoi and Lao Cai. These are trains SP1, SP3 and SP7 to Lao Cai, and SP2, SP4 and SP8 to Hanoi. The preferred journey (and the one used by *Victoria Express*, see right) is on the SP3 train departing each evening at 10 p.m., which arrives in Lao Cai at 6.05 a.m. From Lao Cai, the daily SP4 train departs Lao Cai at 9.40 p.m. and arrives in Hanoi the next morning at 5.30 a.m. Train SP8 from Lao Cai to Hanoi (1.50 p.m./8.50 p.m.) is the only train that offers a view for most of its journey.

NOSTALGIC SLEEPER CARRIAGES

Travellers who appreciate extra comfort should consider travelling with one of several companies that offer private sleeper berths in dedicated carriages coupled to a regular train. While most offer a very similar product to the soft sleepers in Vietnam Railways sleepers, *Victoria Express* berths are a cut above the rest. Passengers who have booked to stay in the hotel can travel in these dedicated carriages. The berths are managed by Vietnam's Victoria Hotels and Resorts, and are housed in two carriages accommodating 48 passengers in shared or private compartments. The configuration is two or four air-conditioned berths. These provide a restful night with the added comfort of reading lights, amenities kit, slippers, drinking water, light refreshments, wi-fi and restroom access. *Victoria Express* guests have access to a lounge at Hanoi Station (open from 7 p.m. to 9.30 p.m.) and complimentary breakfast at the Victoria Sapa Resort and Spa.

NORTH ASIA

INTRODUCTION

North Asia's rail networks include exhilarating journeys through China, Hong Kong, Japan, Mongolia, South Korea and Taiwan.

CHINA

According to the International Union of Railways, China has the world's second longest rail network, with 146,300 km (90,907 miles). The largest rail network is in the USA, with 202,500 km (125,828 miles). Some 72 per cent is electrified and the country has 38,000 km (23,612 miles) of high-speed rail, with another 15,000 km (9,321 miles) under construction. China has the world's biggest high-speed network and is currently developing a high-speed Maglev train with a top speed of 600 km/h (373 mph). The high-speed network conveys two billion passengers annually. Being the most populous nation, with 1.3 billion people, rail transportation is important for both passengers and freight. The network is operated by the state-owned China State Railway Group Company (China Railway, or CRRC), which has 21 main companies responsible for covering specific areas.

There are numerous opportunities to discover China by rail, and the fact that the country really only opened to tourists in the 1970s makes its achievements quite remarkable. Railways traverse climatic extremes and varied topography, from deserts to snow-capped mountains, and from land below sea level to wuthering heights including the world's highest railway. Turfan is 150 m (492 ft) below sea level, while Tanggula Pass on the Lhasa route is 5,068 m (16,627 ft) above sea level. China also operates trains to Mongolia, Russia, Kazakhstan, North Korea and Vietnam. In 2017 it tested freight transportation from China to London as part of the nation's Belt and Road Initiative.

With China's rapid progress, it would appear that it is only a matter of time before it has the world's largest railway network.

HONG KONG

The former British colony and now Chinese Special Administrative Region is home to 7.5 million residents, many of whom regularly use trains. Hong Kong has an efficient public transport system centred on rail and light rail networks. Since 1982, the government-owned Kowloon-Canton Railway Corporation (KCRC) has operated these networks. In 2007, KCRC granted a service concession to the Mass Transit Railway Corporation Limited (MTR) to operate these lines. MTR oversees 10 lines and 95 stations, plus 68 light rail stops. The Airport Express is one such line that provides a seamless connection to the airport.

International trains once terminated near the Peninsula Hotel, but all that remains of this famous building is its clock tower. Since 2016, MTR has provided high-speed rail connectivity to Mainland China's high-speed network from Hong Kong West Kowloon Station to cities like Guangzhou, Shenzhen, Shanghai and Beijing.

The Peak Tram rises 396 m (1,300 ft) from Central to the highest point on Hong Kong's main island. It began service in 1888, making it one of world's oldest funiculars. It carries six million passengers annually, and recent infrastructure improvements enable a faster and more comfortable journey in tramcars that can each transport 210 passengers.

JAPAN

Japan's rail network is one of the world's most comprehensive in providing fast, efficient and punctual but expensive services to many destinations on the four main islands of Honshu, Hokkaido, Kyushu and Shikoku. Service is provided by 100 private companies, while seven Japan Railways Group (JR) companies, which have been privatized since 1987, provide the bulk of the services. Many locals, especially in Greater Tokyo, use trains daily, and most of the world's busiest stations are Japanese.

Compared to many other nations Japan was a late developer, with the first railway between Tokyo and Yokohama opening in 1872. A 1,067 mm (3 ft 6 in) gauge was chosen and is still retained in many parts of Japan on what is known as the classic network. Local, rapid express and limited express trains operate on this gauge. *Shinkansen* (meaning new trunk line) high-speed trains (bullet trains), first introduced in 1964 on 1,435 mm (4 ft 8½ in) standard gauge, can travel at speeds of up to 300 km/h (186 mph). Each *Shinkansen* has its own name, which often incorporates the departure and arrival stations. Many networks are electrified and

Opposite A sixth generation of funicular trams now operates on the Peak Tram on the island of Hong Kong.

Maglev technology has been adopted – SC Maglev, a magnetic levitation railway operated by Central Japan Railway Company, travelled at 603 km/h (370 mph) in 2015 to set a world record.

Some important Japanese train terminology to know includes *Nozomi* (express), *Kodama* (all stations), *Hikari* (semi-fast) and *Mizuho* (specific *Shinkansen* routes). Purchasing a Japan Rail Pass is recommended as it is a cheaper than buying sector tickets, although the pass cannot be used on trains like *Nozomi* and *Mizuho*.

MONGOLIA

The Mongolian network comprises 1,815 km (1,128 miles) of broad-gauge track, with 1,110 km (690 miles) being the main north–south link from Russia, through Mongolia, to China.

The single-track *Trans-Mongolian Railway* (page 18) heads south from the Trans-Siberian Railway and through the Mongolian capital of Ulan Batar on its journey south to Erenhot, just inside the Chinese border. The other substantive but separate section is of 240 km (149 miles) in Eastern Mongolia, with a link through to the Russian network. Some other lines branch east to west from the main line. The rail gauge is the same as Russia's, but a different one is used in China, which means that all carriages must have their bogies changed at the border.

Existing tracks are owned and operated by Ulaanbaatar Railway, which is jointly owned by the governments of Mongolia and Russia. Both governments plan to extend the network, with Mongolian Railway (wholly owned by the Mongolian government) building any extensions. The Zuunbayan to Tavan Tolgoi railway (in the south Gobi Desert), 416 km (258 miles) in length, opened in 2021 principally to transport coal from the world's largest untapped deposits. Mongolia is also interested in working with China in developing export facilities in the Chinese port of Tianjin on the Bohai and Yellow Seas.

The Mongolian Railway History Museum is located within walking distance of the capital's railway station. There are six loco-motives displayed – three steam- and three diesel-powered units.

SOUTH KOREA

Korea's first railway was the Seoul and Chemulpo Railway (now Jemulpo), which opened in 1897. The concession, operated during the colonial era, was granted to two American entrepreneurs and it became fully operational by 1900. Others opened later and Korean National Railway was split into KORAIL and Korea Rail (KR) in 1963. Korial manages the operations and KR maintains

the tracks. Expansion occurred with increased double-tracking and electrification, especially along the main corridor from the capital Seoul to Busan, the second largest city and principal port. High-speed trains were introduced in the 1980s on key lines, including the famous *Blue Train* from Seoul to Busan on what is known as the Gyeonghu Line. Another high-speed rail is the Honam Line, which branches off the Gyeonghu Line at Daejeon to connect to Mokpo.

The Korea Train Express (KTX) is the pride of the fleet and has adopted French TGV/LGV technology. Operations began in 2004 with a top operating speed of 305 km/h (190 mph). Super Rapid Train (SRT) is another train operator that uses KTX-style trains from South Seoul (Gangham) to Busan and Mokpo. ITX trains are semi-fast trains used on select routes. There is a plan to increase South Korea's rail network from 4,274 km (2,656 miles) to 5,137 km (3,192 miles) by 2030 to ensure that no two places are more than two hours apart. Seoul was the first Korean city to intro-duce a subway and now the country's six largest cities have them.

Travellers can enjoy a multi-day journey to select destinations on a Luxury Cruise Train operated by Korail and Rail Cruise Haerang. The trains have cabin accommodation for two, three or four passengers, and offer three itineraries of two- or three-day duration. While complimentary snacks and beverages are served on the train, meals are taken in restaurants along the way.

Korean trains are crowded during January's Lunar New Year celebrations and April's Cherry Blossom Festival. While the border is closed, reunification with North Korea is always a possibility and rail connectivity has already been surveyed.

TAIWAN

Taiwan Railway operates a rail network 2,225 km (1,258 miles) long that basically loops around the island to connect all principal locations. The railway was introduced in 1891, and a high-speed line opened in 2007. Thirteen conventional lines are operated by Taiwan Railway using 1,067 mm (3 ft 6 in) gauge, and covering 1,065 km (662 miles). Trains service 228 stations and operate at speeds of up to 152 km/h (95 mph). A high-speed line operated by the privately owned Taiwan High Speed Rail, of 350 km (217 miles), services west-coast destinations including Nanyang, Taipei, Zuoying and Kaohsiung. It has adopted Japanese technology and operates on 1,435 mm (4 ft 8½ in) gauge to enable a maximum speed of 300 km/h (186 mph). Seating includes business class (four seats across) and standard class (five seats across), with seats A

and E in both classes being window seats.

Taiwan's major cities have metro systems, with the Taipei Mass Rapid Transit (MRT) being the main one in the country. Work began on the system in 1988 and the first section was completed in 1996. There are now 131 stations along six lines and some two million passenger trips are made daily. These lines radiate outwards from a central hub and all have alleviated traffic congestion in an efficient manner, although peak hours are very congested at the busiest stations.

There are two heritage railway systems of interest to enthusiasts – Taiwan Sugar Railways and Taiwan Forest Railways.

Above The Donghae Line in South Korea connects Busanjin and Yeongdeok.

Various Sugar Railways operating on 762 mm (2 ft 6 in) gauge are located in central and southern Taiwan, while Forest Railways at higher altitudes in central Taiwan are popular heritage railways. The longest is the narrow-gauge Alishan Forest Railway of 86 km (53 miles). Its 'Z'-shaped switchbacks, 77 wooden bridges and 50 tunnels ensure tourism interest. While diesel locomotives are mostly used on this route, occasionally a Shay steam locomotive will do the hauling.

CHINA
BEIJING TO HONG KONG VIA GUANGZHOU

ONE COUNTRY, TWO SYSTEMS

Train travellers have been able to travel from Beijing to Hong Kong (Kowloon) via Guangzhou since 1996. China's rail landscape is changing rapidly and this is no more evident than on this line.

Before taking this journey, passengers can arrive in Beijing all the way from Europe to begin the trip on continuous track using trains like the *Trans-Mongolian Railway* (page 18).

The journey from Beijing provides a convenient link between the Chinese capital and the strategically located destinations of Guangzhou and Hong Kong. This connection also ensures its popularity for those seeking to continue beyond the Special Administrative Region of Hong Kong to Hanoi (page 114), then from the Vietnamese capital to numerous parts of Southeast Asia.

The journey from Beijing to Guangzhou/Hong Kong offers three different experiences – high-speed train, classic train and high-speed sleeper train. The fastest provides passengers with the opportunity to experience China's new breed of trains and to get a snapshot of the countryside. The classic train enables passengers to travel over a 24-hour period and enjoy a comfortable sleeping compartment, while the third option is a combination of these two trains but with a change of train in Guangzhou.

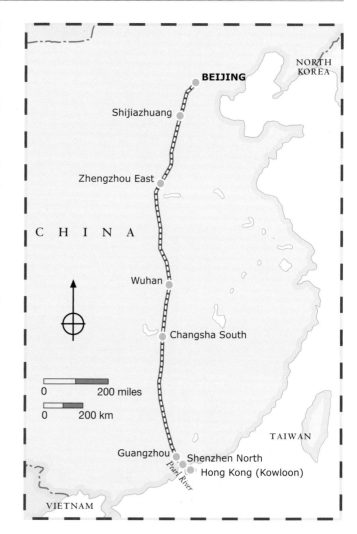

TRACK NOTES

High-speed *Fuxing* trains (bullet trains), the fastest and most expensive option, cover the 2,441 km (1,516 miles) in less than nine hours. Opened in 2018, this service operating on electrified dual tracks departs from Beijing West Station and travels at an average speed of 300 km/h (186 mph). The train departs after breakfast and arrives in Hong Kong for dinner on the same day, while making several stops. These include Shijiazhuang, Zhengzhou East, Wuhan, Changsha South, Guangzhou and Shenzhen North, before the train terminates at Hong Kong's West Kowloon Station.

Construction began in 2005 and was completed by 2012. The Shenzhen to Hong Kong section was completed in 2015. The rolling stock used is CRH380-AL, comprising 14 multiple units and traction units at both ends. The train extends over 400 m (1,312 ft), has a small cafe counter and can accommodate up to 1,066 passengers.

Classic trains cover the distance in 24 hours and they are recommended for those seeking the cheapest option, plus the opportunity to spend a comfortable night on a train that includes a restaurant car serving Chinese meals. Soft- and hard-class sleepers are available.

The third option is the high-speed sleeper train that departs on several days of the week. Passengers seamlessly change from their D-category high-speed sleeper train at Guangzhou before continuing on to Hong Kong.

WELCOME ABOARD

Travellers should allocate several days in Beijing to explore all that the capital offers before travelling south. The Imperial Palace, or Forbidden City Complex, of pavilions, halls, courtyard gardens and walls, covers 73 ha (180 acres) enclosed within a protective

Above West Kowloon Station is the Hong Kong terminus for the Guangzhou–Shenzhen–Hong Kong Express Rail Link.

moat. It was off limits to commoners for 500 years, but now visitors are welcome to China's largest and best-preserved historic precinct. It was the imperial court for 24 emperors from the Ming Dynasty in the fifteenth century until the Qing Dynasty in 1911. It lies adjacent to the vast expanse of Tiananmen Square, the world's largest public square.

The Old Summer Palace of lakes, palaces and gardens is another enchanting attraction. Built in the eighteenth and nineteenth centuries, this UNESCO World Heritage Site is dominated by Kunming Lake and Longevity Hill. Visitors can also explore Houhai District, a neighbourhood with many well-preserved heritage buildings, courtyards and alleyways, or *hutong*s.

Most visitors head to the Great Wall, a symbol of China's strength and power. It was built section by section over 2,000 years to protect the land from northern nomadic marauders. Sections unite to extend more than 6,035 km (3,750 miles), but the most visited section is at Badaling, while Mutianyu and Simatai see fewer visitors.

Travellers for Hong Kong depart from Beijing West Station, which is accessible from the city by metro trains. Seating/sleepers depend on the train selected – high-speed trains offer second-, first- and business-class seats. The first two classes have two seats on either side of an aisle, while business class has just three seats across, with one on one side of the aisle and two on the other. Business-class seats can be extended to flatbed sleepers, and a hot meal and continuous non-alcoholic beverages are served. They also have access to lounges in Beijing and Hong Kong, although facilities are limited.

Classic train travellers can select from deluxe soft sleepers, soft sleepers and hard sleepers. Two sleeping berths are enclosed in deluxe soft-sleeper compartments with lockable doors. Some compartments have a private toilet, and all provide pillows, blankets, luggage racks and power points. Soft-class sleepers are similar but accommodate four passengers, with two lower and two upper berths. Hard-class sleepers accommodate six passengers, but the door cannot be locked.

The first stop is Shijiazhuang (Shimen), the capital of Hebei Province, with a population of 11 million people. Unusually, both high-speed and conventional trains use the new Shijiazhuang Station constructed in 2012. In addition to having numerous temples, parks and an ancient stone bridge, visitors can alight here to visit Boadu Village with a fortified hilltop village and an ancient Buddha statue on Mount Cangyan.

Zhengzhou East Station, the second stop, is a junction for the Xuzhou to Lanzhou Railway. Trains also branch off from here to Shanghai, Nanjing and Hangzhou.

Wuhan, the capital of Hubei Province, is the next stop. This city of 11 million people is situated at the confluence of the Yangtze and Han Rivers. These are important for transportation, and Wuhan is one of China's four key rail hubs. There are three main railway stations and all are located well apart, although there are

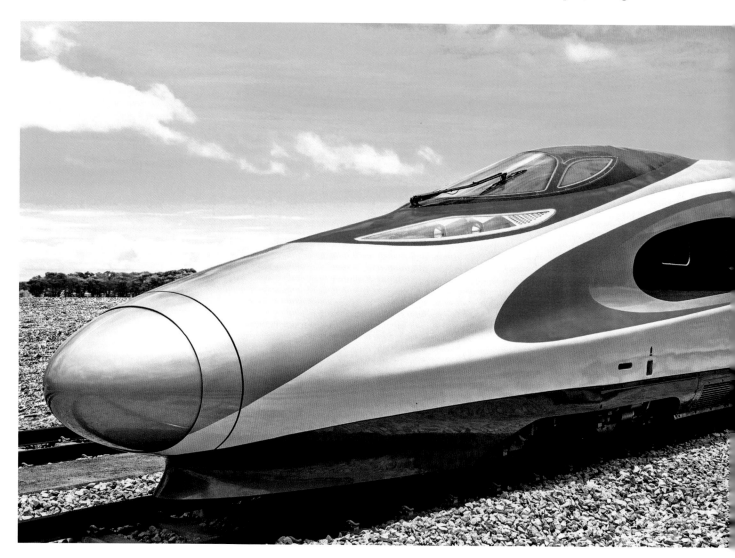

plans to link them via the city's mass transit of nine lines and 228 stations. The train pulls into the new Wuhan Railway Station of 11 platforms. High-speed trains to Shanghai depart from Hankou Railway Station and take under six hours to reach their destination. Wuhan has many tourist attractions, including lakes, parks, museums, a theme park, Yellow Crane Tower, large seafood market and various shopping precincts, while the mighty Three Gorges Dam is located upriver.

The section of track from Wuhan to Guangzhou accommodates reportedly the world's fastest commercial train at 394 km/h (245 mph). The next stop is Changsha South Station in Yuhua District of Changsha, a city of 10 million people. The station is also on the high-speed rail link between Shanghai and Kunming, and a Maglev line (magnetic levitation) connects to the airport. The capital of Hunan Province is home to numerous universities, as well as an international culture and arts centre, Meixi Lake and museums.

The last stop before Hong Kong is Guangzhou (Canton), located on the Pearl River Delta near where the river enters the South China Sea. With a population exceeding 15 million people, Guangzhou has numerous attractions, including Canton Tower, medicinal markets, Sun Yat Sen Memorial Hall, shopping precincts and Shamian, the city's old trading compound.

The through train passes Guangzhou East Station before travelling the 120 km (75 miles) to Kowloon West Station. Here, Hong Kong has its own border and immigration procedures and a separate currency to China, although this divide is narrowing. Hong Kong's deep-water harbour is a major attraction, and taking a ferry from Kowloon to Central is an essential activity. One of the world's steepest funiculars from Central rises to Victoria Peak at 552 m (1,811 ft) above sea level. Work commenced on the railway in 1888, and now the peak is wonderful for views of the islands scattered across the South China Sea.

ATTENTION TO DETAIL

Passengers need to arrive at least 45 minutes before the train departs, because the stations are large and could be complicated for novices, and bags need to be scanned. Tickets can be purchased 28 days before departure from Beijing, and 60 days before Hong Kong departures.

Trains on the Kowloon to Canton Railway connect through to mainland China. This network has operated as part of Hong Kong's Mass Transit Railway Corporation Limited (MTR) since 2007. Other international trains depart from Hong Kong and head through China and on to Hanoi, Vietnam.

For a country as vast as China, visitors have to be judicious in their train selection, unless time is no obstacle. Seeking the assistance of companies specializing in train travel is also advisable for those in a hurry or new to Asian travel.

China Railway's plan is to have 155 pairs of high-speed trains operating on the Beijing to Guangzhou line.

Left Some 30 pairs of high-speed trains operating daily between West Kowloon and Guangzhou South cover the 142 km (88 miles) in about one hour.

BEIJING TO URUMQI

RETRACING THE SILK ROAD

Travellers have been traversing various Silk Road routes from Europe to Asia for centuries. Urumqi in Western China is on one of these routes, and travellers can retrace parts of the Silk Road on the railway from Beijing to Urumqi, the capital of Xinjiang Uighur Autonomous Province, and even on to neighbouring Kazakhstan.

Silk and other precious commodities were conveyed by camel caravans between the East and the West along several routes, over mountains and across inhospitable deserts. Marco Polo travelled these fabled 'superhighways' between present-day Mongolia, Russia, Iran (Persia), India and various Mediterranean countries. While some routes date back two millennia, the Venetian merchant travelled through China in the thirteenth century. Xi'an, at the eastern end of one Silk Road route, is 6,700 km (4,200 miles) from the Mediterranean.

The various Silk Roads were popular until the fifteenth century, when maritime routes opened, making the ancient overland paths less appealing. Interestingly, the term Silk Road was first used in the nineteenth century.

Western China has more in common with Central Asian countries like Kyrgyzstan, Kazakhstan and Tajikistan than the rest of China. Xinjiang is home to ethnic minorities including Muslim Uighurs (Uyghurs) as the dominant group. Uighurs are regarded as an official minority group of 12 million who live in Xinjiang. There are another 12 minority groups, including Tajiks, Kirgiz, Uzbeks and Kazaks.

Travel in this part of China is like visiting another country, with a vast desert stretching over 1,000 km (621 miles) and Central Asia steppes above which snow-capped mountains rise to create a starkly contrasting landscape. It is the most arid part of China, with the nation's both coldest and hottest parts, and Lake Aydingkul, the world's second lowest lake. The Turfan Basin is the hottest place in China and not a welcoming destination for summer exploration. Timing is important for those planning to sightsee as winter is equally harsh, with temperatures below zero.

Western China is also culturally fascinating, including abandoned desert cities and places where different languages are spoken,

and people write in different scripts, follow different religions and consume exotic foods.

TRACK NOTES

High-speed trains connect from Beijing to Urumqi, but other trains also operate to make it a good line to alight from for those wishing to sightsee along the journey of 3,046 km (1,893 miles). The first railway to Urumqi was completed in 1963, while high-speed trains entered service in 2014. The railway passes through the harsh lands of Western China, where sandstorms once buried the tracks and where in 2007 strong winds derailed a train.

When author Paul Theroux travelled here in the 1980s, the train from Peking (as Beijing was then known) to Urumqi was China's longest railway journey: four and a half days through mountains and deserts. A fellow passenger called the train the 'The Iron Rooster'. The fastest train now covers the distance in 35½ hours.

WELCOME ABOARD

This journey can begin in numerous eastern cities and end in Urumqi. From here, intrepid travellers can continue on to other

Above The multitude of sculptured terracotta soldiers depicting the army of the first Emperor of China are the main tourist attraction in Xi'an.

exotic destinations like Kashgar (Kashi) or fabled Samarkand, Bukhara, Khiva and Tashkent in neighbouring countries. Trains to Urumqi depart from Beijing and Beijing West Stations, and travellers need to check times before setting off. There are two stations in Urumqi, too – Urumqi and Urumqi South.

The train passes through Zhengzhou, Luoyang and Huashan before pulling into Xi'an. A chance to see the Terracotta Army of 8,000 life-size soldiers, displaying striking realism in battle formation, is the main reason to break the journey in Xi'an. The army dates back 2,300 years and was erected for Emperor Qin Shi Huang, who feared enemies in his afterlife. The army was discovered in 1924 by a farmer ploughing his field.

Lanzhou, the capital of Gansu Province, is strategically located along the Yellow River, and is considered to be at the edge of the 'outer limits' and the beginning of Islamic China. It is also the beginning of the Lanxin, or Lanzhou, to Xinjiang High-speed Rail Line of 31 stations along 1,776 km (1,104 miles) of double-track,

electrified railway. The new line opened in 2014 and is much shorter than the original track of 1,903 km (1,182 miles), which is now mostly used for freight. The new route deviates through Qinghai Province, thus shortening the line.

Further west, Jiayaguan is an ancient Han Chinese outpost, considered the Great Wall's western extremity since 1372. The Gates of Enlightenment and Conciliation plus the watchtower of Jiayaguan Fort are the main attractions. The backdrop is the snow-capped Qilianshan peaks, where walking on the 1 July Glacier at an altitude of 4,300 m (14,108 ft) can appeal to adventurous travellers. While much of this journey passes through barren landscapes referred to as the dead centre of Asia, sheep graze on some mountainous pasturelands.

Dunhuang is another stop to consider in order to visit the Mogao Caves, one of China's great artistic treasures with its Buddhist frescoes and sculptures. There are 500 caves but not all are accessible. Sadly, much of the artwork has been plundered, with some artefacts now housed in the British Museum. The world's highest sand dunes are close to Dunhuang.

Several oases within the parched west have been important caravan stops and market towns for 2,000 years. Both Hami and Turfan are accessible by train. They are located below sea level and receive little rainfall. However, the harnessing of underground water led to their development. While water did not guarantee the future of these oases, without it they were doomed. Here, crops are cultivated, with Hami being where the highly prized Hami melons are grown.

Turfan, a green basin situated 150 m (492 ft) below sea level, is China's lowest point. This became an important oasis town when the melting snow from the Bogdashan Mountains was harnessed via *karez*, an above- and below-ground irrigation network 5,000 km (3,107 miles) long, which has been used to green the desert (known as the *gobi*, or waterless place) for some 2,000 years. Many regard this hand-hewn system as rivalling the Great Wall. Grapes are grown here on trellises, then dried to make raisins. Apricots are also grown and dried to make ideal food for crossing the desert. These products and decorated knives, Muslim apparel and carpets abound in Turfan's market.

Turfan is also the train stop for the lost city of Gaocheng (Karakhoja). The former Silk Road city, founded in the seventh century, was once a centre for Buddhism before conversion to Islam. Gaocheng, once a powerful city with tall walls surrounded by a moat, is now a dusty ruin. Other attractions in the district

are Flaming Mountain and Bezeklik Buddha Caves, Grape Valley and Jiaohe Ruins.

Turfan is just 160 km (100 miles) south-east of Urumqi, or one-hour's travel by high-speed train. For those who like cultural variety in a small town, Turfan is far more appealing than Urumqi. Trains also connect from Turfan to Kashgar.

Urumqi is the last large Chinese city before Almaty in Kazakhstan. Attractions in the city include a museum, Renmin Park, Hongshan Park and Red Hill Pagoda. Located 115 km (71 miles) east of Urumqi, Tainchi (Heavenly Lake) resembles the Swiss Alps, and at 1,900 m (6,234 ft), its snow-capped mountains and turquoise lakes are very picturesque. Kazakh yurts and colourful horses can be seen, as can Bogda Feng, which dominates the skyline at 5,445 m (17,864 ft).

The railway also extends 1,475 km (917 miles) south-west to Kashgar, a market town with a lively Sunday bazaar that attracts many visitors. Located at the foot of the Pamir Mountains on the western fringe of the forbidding Taklamakan Desert (one of the world's largest and remotest deserts), Kashgar has been a strategic

Each train consists of eight carriages extending some 214 m (700 ft) in length. The configuration is five power cars and three trailers, including two first-class carriages, five second-class carriages and one dining car. Almost 44 train sets travel the island daily from 6.40 a.m. to 10.04 p.m. in each direction. The fastest train, Train D7339 in the early evening, takes 87 minutes to travel from Haikou Dong (East) to Sanya, hitting a maximum speed of 220 km/h (137 mph). The slowest train takes two and a half hours to cover the distance.

WELCOME ABOARD

There are 15 stations on the East Coast and 16 on the West Coast, with the main stations being Hainan Meilan Airport (the air gateway), Haikou, East Haikou (where many trains terminate), Yalong Bay and Sanya.

Hainan's tropical climate ensures its popularity with holidaymakers, who mostly head to the Sanya-Yalong strip in the south of the island. The journey takes some two hours from the main airport near Haikou. The main sandy stretch in the south is Dadonghai Beach, close to Sanya city centre. Less than 25 years ago, all that existed here was the beach, occasional swaying palms and the surf. Now it is lined with high-rise hotels, restaurants, bars and watersport activities. It is the district's most popular beachfront, although neighbouring Yalong Bay is close behind it.

Above Some 170 pairs of high-speed trains travel daily between Sanya and Haikou on the island of Hainan.

While most visitors stay along the beachfront, the city of Sanya has a lively downtown with an evening market and a pub street. The train station is centrally located in the city. Some other attractions in the south include Nanshan Temple, Yanoda Rainforest Cultural Tourism Zone, Xinglong Tropical Botanical Gardens and Nanwan Monkey Island. In Haikou or the north, visit the Volcanic Cluster Global Geopark (with two volcanoes), Mission Hills Huayi Brothers Xiaogang Movie Town, Hainan Museum and Quilou Old Street in Haikou. Golf played on some 20 courses attracts many tourists. Mission Hills Hainan is one of the world's largest golf complexes.

The island is the original home of several minority groups, who mostly live in the mountainous interior and beyond the reach of train travel but not public transport.

ATTENTION TO DETAIL

Tickets can be purchased 30 days in advance from booking counters or vending machines at stations. Travel is now ticketless, with passport scanners at automatic gates to platforms verifying the traveller, the train and the seat number. Smoking is not permitted on Chinese high-speed trains.

QINGHAI TO LHASA

ROOF OF THE WORLD

The Qinghai to Lhasa route in China's Tibet Autonomous Region currently operates on the world's highest railway. The loftiest point on the Xining-Golmud-Lhasa train is at Tanggula, 5,068 m (16,627 ft) above sea level. By comparison, Europe's highest railway is Switzerland's Jungfrau (3,454 m/11,332 ft), in South America it is Peru's Lima to Huancayo Railway (4,783 m/15,692 ft), and in North America it is at Leadville Colorado on the Colorado and Southern Railroad (3,414 m/11,201 ft).

In July 2006 the first train from Xining in Qinghai traversed the Kunlun Range on its journey to Lhasa. It had been possible to travel as far as Golmud for some time, with work on the difficult extension to Lhasa only beginning in 2001. Tibet has always been the largest topographical barrier to Trans-Asia communications, but the new railway effectively integrated isolated Tibet into the rest of China. While the train passes through some of China's wildest but most beautiful landscapes, the wilderness was not as impenetrable as Theroux had predicted.

Tourism to Tibet (Xizang in Chinese) was also a big motivator for engineers to identify the Lhasa route. While Tibet is the world's highest and largest plateau, fabled Lhasa is located in a basin surrounded by mountains. At 3,650m (11,975 ft), the Tibetan capital is also known as the Forbidden City, and is considered one of the world's highest cities.

The Chinese invaded (what China calls 'the peaceful liberation

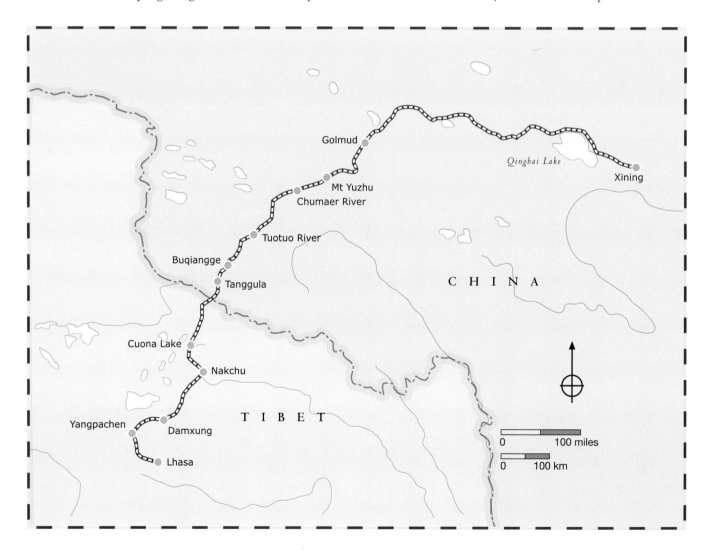

of Tibet from feudal serfdom') Tibet in 1949, then annexed it as part of China in 1959.

Tibet is also ecologically important for hundreds of millions of people downstream because it is the source of some of the world's greatest and most sacred rivers, like the Yangtze, Yellow, Salween, Mekong, Brahmaputra, Ayeyarwady, Indus and Ganges.

TRACK NOTES

The line of 1,956 km (1.215 miles) all the way from Xining to Lhasa opened in 2006, thus enabling more tourists to visit the mythical Himalayan Shangri-La. What was once one of the world's remotest outposts, accessible only by air or an arduous road journey, has become one of China's most coveted travel destinations. In parts, the train travels at altitudes exceeding 5,000 m (16,404 ft) where

Above Also known as the 'Sky Road', the train to Lhasa passes through a variety of landscapes from vivid red mountains to snow-covered peaks.

the air is so thin that oxygen is added to the train's ventilation for passenger comfort. Carriages are also sealed like aircraft to help protect passengers from altitude sickness.

The line's construction has been referred to as the world's most ambitious railway project because it traverses a challenging high plateau with a section of substratum of permafrost exceeding 500 km (311 miles) in length. The annual freezing and thawing of this permafrost causes dramatic shifts and was just one of many challenges engineers confronted. High winds, earthquakes and predicting changing conditions due to global warming were some of the other factors. They also had to address environmental

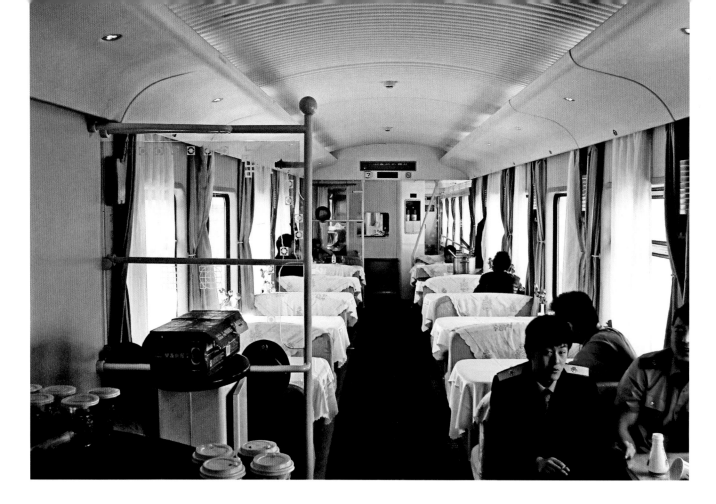

concerns about the train traversing such sensitive ecosystems.

The train to Golmud travels at speeds of up to 140 km/h (89 mph), while the journey beyond Golmud is slower, at 100 km/h (62 mph). Onboard facilities on the six daily overnight Z Class trains include sleepers and a restaurant car. The journey takes between 20 and 22 hours.

WELCOME ABOARD

Travellers can join the Lhasa train at Xining in landlocked Qinghai Province in China's central west. However, long-distance travellers can arrive in Xining from other cities, including Beijing, Xi'an and Chengdu. The Lanqing Railway operates normal and high-speed trains between Lanzhou, Gansu and Xining. Normal trains between Beijing and Xining take between 18 and 24 hours.

Qinghai is a popular destination with local holidaymakers especially during the summer months of July and August, when the region's mild weather makes it very appealing. Its weather contrasts to many other parts of China and appeals to travellers who come to admire attractions like Dongguan Mosque, Kumbum Buddhist Monastery and the Tibetan Medicine and Culture Museum.

The train passes Qinghai Lake (Qinghai Hu) in the distance.

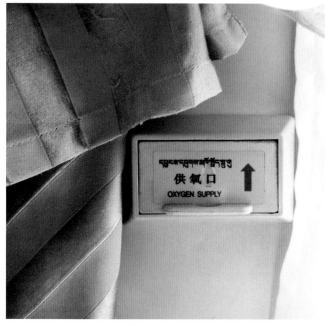

Top The dining car serves Chinese and Tibetan meals, three times per day.

Above Trains are air-conditioned and pressurized like a plane. They include an oxygen supply, which effectively alleviates altitude sickness by increasing the train's oxygen content.

This is China's largest saltwater lake despite being located thousands of kilometres from the sea. It measures 105 km (65 miles) by 63 km (39 miles) and is particularly attractive in summer, when it is surrounded by yellow rape flowers. Its birdlife is prolific and activities include boating and cycling.

Golmud is located in the wild and stony Qinghai Desert, with Lhasa another 1,142 km (710 miles) down the line. The train passes what many consider to be China's most beautiful landscapes, of white ridges and snow-capped pinnacles, wild rivers frozen in winter and flowing turbulently in summer, remote farmhouses, and ecologically significant marshlands and grasslands where yaks and Tibetan Antelope graze. It traverses the high-altitude Tibetan plateau, where temperatures often plummet to below zero. It was these undisturbed and extreme ecosystems that raised the concerns of environmentalists when the railway was proposed. This is the landscape that James Hilton fictionalized as Shangri-La in his novel *Lost Horizon*.

After many hours the train terminates in Lhasa, situated at 3,650m (11,975 ft) above sea level. The station is located 6 km (4 miles) from downtown Lhasa, and is a modernist representation of the famous Potala Palace. Lhasa in the Tibetan language means 'Holy City', or 'Place of the Gods'.

While Lhasa, with a population of 400,000 people, is a holy place for pilgrims, it is also a market town. This magical and once mystical city was the Dalai Lama's former seat of power in independent Tibet. He escaped Lhasa in 1959 with tens of thousands of devotees and is now in enforced exile in Dharamsala, India. While displaying his image is prohibited in Tibet, His Holiness is still revered by many Tibetans.

The Potala Palace on Mount Marpori is the 13-storey-high former winter palace of the Dalai Lama. This imposing palace with red-and-white walls and glistening golden roofs dominates the Lhasa skyline. It has some 1,000 rooms, and before skyscrapers was the world's tallest building. It is considered one of the world's great architectural wonders, and visitor numbers to what is now basically a museum have been capped for its protection. Visitors now admire the palace, which was completed in 1653, although on seventh-century foundations. Nearby, Norbulingka was the Dalai Lama's summer residence.

The city's spiritual heart is actually Jokhang Temple in the market district known as Barkhor. This golden-roofed temple enclosing some 200 Buddha statues is more than 1,300 years old and displays an eclectic mix of Chinese, Tibetan, Indian and Nepalese architecture. It is considered Tibet's holiest Buddhist shrine, where devotees prostrate themselves to gain religious merit. Barkor is a rabbit warren of side streets leading from the main square. Traditional Tibetan houses are preserved here within a sea of Chinese modernity.

Drepung Monastery just outside Lhasa was, in the seventeenth century, the world's largest monastery, with 10,000 monks residing and studying here.

ATTENTION TO DETAIL

In addition to a Chinese visa, foreigner travellers heading to Tibet require a Tibet Travel Permit (also known as an Alien's Travel Permit). This is issued by the Tibet Tourism Bureau and is normally handled by travel agents. Independent travel is not permitted in Tibet, and travellers need to use the services of a travel company or travel guide.

New train lines are opening to and from Lhasa. In addition to lines from the capital and major eastern seaboard cities, a new line connecting Lhasa to Nyingchi in the south-east of Tibet (close to the border with the Indian state of Arunachal Pradesh) opened recently. This section of 435 km (270 miles) of electrified, single-track rail is known as the Lalin Railway and is part of the larger Sichuan-Tibet Railway of 1,838 km (1,142 miles), which is still under construction. A new fleet of Fuxing Plateau bi-modal multiple-train units capable of operating on electrified and non-electrified track uses this line. These 12-car sets were designed by China Railway to operate under Tibet's extreme climatic conditions. Each set has a power unit at either end and can transport 755 passengers in first, second and commercial class. Some 90 per cent of the journey takes places at higher than 3,000 m (9,843 ft), and oxygen is provided at higher latitudes and in long tunnels (at an altitude of 3,500 m / 11,483 ft, the amount of oxygen in the air is 35 per cent less than at sea level). This rail service halves the road journey to Nyingchi. Adventurous travellers may want to make the two-day drive across the Friendship Highway from Tibet to Nepal.

Many Tibetan observers have noted that Tibet managed to preserve much of its culture because of its isolation and because it was so difficult to access. The railway changed all of that and Tibet's assimilation into the rest of China is now inevitable. Michael Palin in his 2004 book *Himalaya* noted '… the fact remains that the railway is likely to change Tibet as much as anything in its history'.

JAPAN
SHINKANSEN

BULLET TRAINS

The first Japanese *Shinkansen* ('new main line') was the world's first purpose-built super-high-speed railway. Built to serve one of the most heavily populated and most industrialized areas of the world, this new separate railway, free from grade crossings and other direct interference, allowed Japanese Railways (JR) to augment services on its very busy Tokaido route between Tokyo and Osaka.

The *New Tokaido Shinkansen* was opened in October 1964, so was fully operational in time for the Japan World Exposition, Expo '70, staged in Osaka in 1970. The initial route of 515 km (320 miles) connected the centre of Tokyo and Osaka with 10 intermediate stops. Initial service featured 30 round trips a day, running at a maximum speed of 209 km/h (130 mph). The trains were powered by overhead high-voltage AC electric catenary.

The original *Shinkansen* route proved a phenomenal success, as it inspired other high-speed rail systems around the world and stimulated expansion of the Japanese high-speed network. While the New Tokaido awed observers, JR's later *Shinkansen* routes were built to even higher standards, allowing much faster speeds, while the New Tokaido Line was gradually upgraded.

TRACK NOTES

Where the traditional Japanese railway system uses narrow-gauge track of 1,067 mm (3 ft 6 in), the high-speed *Shinkansen* features the 1,435 mm (4 ft 8½ in) standard gauge (common to most railways in Europe and North America). This broader gauge was selected for better lateral stability and to allow for higher capacity trains.

The original 1964-era 'Series 0' trains, typified by their blue-and-white bullet noses, were the internationally renowned 'bullet trains', and they became iconic symbols of Japanese high-speed rail. These reached the end of their lives many years ago, and would be considered slow by today's standards. Since the 1960s much faster trains have been refined, many of which now travel in revenue service at speeds of up to 300 km/h (186 mph), and even faster than that in special test runs. Modern streamlined *Shinkansen* trains are designed with futuristic aerodynamic shapes, and incorporate long, tapered noses, wing-like pantographs (electrical collection devices that draw current from overhead catenary), and pantograph shields to minimize the roar of the train sailing along at top speed.

WELCOME ABOARD

There are currently 10 *Shinkansen* routes, each offering a variety of train services that vary according to their exclusivity, price and scheduled speed. Some services use specially designed high-speed trains, while others use more generic *Shinkansen* trains. These all operate on three of the four main islands, with Shikoku the only one yet to be connected to the high-speed network.

In the late 1970s and early '80s, new lines were built north and east of Tokyo. Primary northern routes divide in the Tokyo suburb of Omiya, with the Tohoku Line running due north towards Morioka, while the Joetsu Line heads north-west towards Niigata. Limited services began in 1982 and additional routes have since been added, while the Tohoku Line was extended to Hachinohe and Aomori. Northern *Shinkansen* trains operate from a separate Tokyo terminus. Although cross-platform transfers can be made today from northern *Shinkansen* Lines to the Tokaido Line at Tokyo Central Station, there is no through service. There are several reasons for this. The first is the assumption that most passengers are destined for Tokyo, Japan's capital and largest city (population more than 35 million people). Secondly, since privatization of the JR network in 1987, the lines are operated by different companies.

Thirdly, there is a lack of connection between the two networks, and operational differences stemming from different voltages used north and south of Tokyo.

The key to the success of *Shinkansen* is its largely tangent route profile, despite Japan's predominantly mountainous terrain. This has been made possible by extensive tunnelling. For example, the Sanyo Line (opened between Shin-Osaka and Okayama in 1972) traverses nearly 56 km (35 miles) of tunnel, representing more than one-third of the line. Northern *Shinkansen* lines also have numerous tunnels: the *Joetsu Shinkansen* is 40 per cent through tunnels, with some sections being exceptionally long, including the famous Daishimizu bore of 22 km (14 miles) in length.

On JR Central and JR East routes (on the Tokaido and Sanyo routes), Nozomi (translated as 'hope' in English) trains are among the fastest. These premier, extra-fare, extra-fast express services between Tokyo and Hakata call for the most advanced train designs, including the ultra-modern Series 700 trains noted for their pronounced platypus-bill front ends. When the older, but equally futuristic, 500-series trains entered Nozomi service in 1997, they were the fastest regularly scheduled trains in the world, and they became virtually an exclusive domain of business executives and the travelling elite.

Below The *Hokkaido Shinkansen* is one of nine bullet trains operating on the islands of Hokkaido, Honshu and Kyushu.

Other modern trains include those for service on northern *Shinkansen* lines. There are double-deck MAX sets. Also, specially designed trains operate off the primary *Shinkansen* network on sinuous routes converted from narrow gauge to standard gauge. Among these are Series 400 trains working the Tsubasa ('wings') services from Tokyo to Yamagata and Shinjo (via the Ou line/ *Yamagata Shinkansen*, which diverges from the Tohoku Line at Fukushima, 256 km/159 miles north of Tokyo Central).

Shinkansen services are expanding throughout Japan. The *Hokkaido Shinkansen*, which now travels via an undersea tunnel between the islands of Honshu and Hokkaido, currently terminates in Hakodate in the south of the northern island. However, work is currently underway on extending this through to Sapporo.

Another line under construction is the line from Tokyo, south-west to Shin-Osaka. The *Hokuriku Shinkansen* is being extended from Kanazawa to Tsuruga, while the *Kyushu Shinkansen* will soon connect to Nagasaki in the far south-west of the island.

ATTENTION TO DETAIL

The best way for travellers to experience the Japanese railway network, including high-speed *Shinkansen* routes, is to purchase a Japan Rail Pass before arrival in Japan. This is valid on most JR trains; however, reservations are required for most *Shinkansen* journeys, and further additional fees apply on Nozomi trains and in private compartments on high-speed services. The high cost of single tickets for *Shinkansen* trains in Japan can make walk-up travel prohibitively expensive without a pass.

Above The best bullet train option is the *Fuji Excursion Limited Express*, which operates from Tokyo's Shinjuku Station to the Kawaguchiko stop.

SEVEN STARS IN KYUSHU

LUXURY TRAVEL ON A SLOW TRAIN

Japan's third largest and southernmost island of Kyushu is home to the nation's slowest but most luxurious train, *Seven Stars in Kyushu*. The train has been nominated by readers of *Condé Naste Traveler* (USA) as the world's best railway journey. While the train's facilities are equal to a highly starred hotel, its name refers to Kyushu's seven prefectures, seven major attractions and its seven carriages. With just 12 guest compartments, the waiting list for a berth on this train operated by JR Kyushu Railway Company (JR Kyushu) is extensive, and travellers need to book months in advance. Attention to detail is a hallmark of the train, the interior of which is meticulously finished in Japanese timber marquetry and parquetry, textiles and ceramics, and where local and Western meals prepared by iconic chefs are culinary masterpieces. The train successfully combines food, culture, nature and nostalgia in all its departures.

TRACK NOTES

The train departs from Hakata Station in Fukuoka, Kyushu's largest city. A DF200-7000 locomotive hauls just seven carriages that accommodate a maximum of 26 passengers. The locomotive is a dedicated class of the DF200-7000 series manufactured by Kawasaki Heavy Industries Rolling Stock Company and normally used for freight haulage. The coaches were made by either Hitachi or JR Kyushu.

Both the locomotive and carriage exteriors are finished in a glistening burgundy livery. Carriages are numbered but depend on the location of the locomotive. When the locomotive is at the front, car one is at the back and houses a lounge and Blue Moon Bar. This car features a floor-to-ceiling panoramic window for views of the passing scenery. Dining car 'Jupiter' is numbered two, while cars three to six have three suites per carriage and car seven at the front has just two deluxe suites that can accommodate up to three passengers each. The location of the front and rear carriages changes depending on the locomotive's positioning.

WELCOME ABOARD

The train offers a four-day, three-night journey and a two-day, one-night departure. Guests meet in the train's dedicated Kinsei Lounge at Hakata Station, before being ushered to their individual air-conditioned compartment with either twin or double bedding, plus an en-suite toilet/shower lined with cypress timber. An all-inclusive mini-bar and wi-fi are available in each suite. After settling in, guests explore the train's public areas, which include a lounge car where a pianist performs, plus the dining car where a magician adds a fun component to dining.

The train passes through forests of colourful hues – which depend on the season – rice fields, bays with fishing trawlers and mountainous streams. Passengers alight at several stops to dine, stay over on one evening in a ryokan (traditional Japanese inn), where they can relax in their own private hot-spring *onsen* (the longer journey only), and tour off-train attractions by luxury coach. One of the highlights is a visit to the Aso volcano, which has a caldera 128 km (80 miles) in circumference, offering panoramic views from the rim over a sea of rice fields surrounding the mountain.

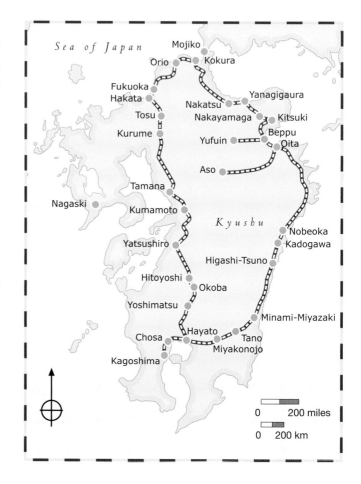

Above Launched in 2013, the *Seven Stars in Kyushu* was Japan's first luxury sleeper train offering unparalleled service.

Menus and chefs change throughout the year, and meals are served on the train or at off-train restaurants along the way. Advanced dietary requirements are accommodated and passengers can enjoy meals such as famous Hakata-style sushi, a meal produced from organically grown ingredients, a French dinner prepared from local seasonal ingredients or a fusion culinary creation from Oita. Various craft activities are conducted on the train for those who do not want to participate in the organized excursions. Complimentary wines, sake, shochu and other premium beverages are recommended by an on-board sommelier.

The locals love the train, and guests receive a warm welcome as they travel throughout the island. Locals are used to seeing the train glide by at its regular time, and come out to wave to train guests. Passengers can enjoy the warm reception and views of the rustic scenery rolling past the panoramic windows.

ATTENTION TO DETAIL

Just as the *Indian Pacific Railway* across Australia is a rite of passage for many Australians, travelling on the *Seven Stars in Kyushu* is a journey many Japanese aspire to take. The two journeys per week are booked out months ahead, but some cabins are reserved on each departure for foreign travellers. Bookings are allocated twice a year via a lottery, and it is best for overseas guests to use an international agent such as Luxury Train Club (UK) to secure a berth. Fares for this train match its exclusivity.

JR Kyushu operates several tourist, resort and excursion trains, and travellers on more modest budgets can discover the island's rich assets using a JR Kyushu Rail Pass that offers unlimited multi-day travel.

ACROSS JAPAN ON THE OLD NETWORK

NARROW-GAUGE HIGHLIGHTS

Japan has one of the most intensively developed railway systems in the world. Visitors touring Japan are well advised to discover the country by using the numerous narrow-gauge lines, as well as the extensive network of *Shinkansen* routes (bullet trains).

TRACK NOTES

Japan's rail network comprises more than 30,625 km (19, 029 miles) of track, of which the vast majority of lines are 1,067 mm (3 ft 6 in) gauge. This is narrow compared to the more common 1,435 mm (4 ft 8½ in) track gauge used by most American and European railways, and by Japan's famous high-speed *Shinkansen*

trains. While the *Shinkansen* network, with its futuristic 'bullet' trains, symbolizes modern Japanese railways, it only covers just over 2,765 km (1,718 miles) of the entire rail system.

Whereas the *Shinkansen* is a straightforward, high-speed, double-track network using some of the world's most impressive railway infrastructure for exclusive operation of very fast passenger trains, the rest of the network is a complex system serving many other types of train and infrastructure. Lines range from multiple-track suburban lines around Tokyo, to the heavily travelled Tokaido and Chuo Lines, which have a mix of local, express passenger and freight trains operating on them. Other

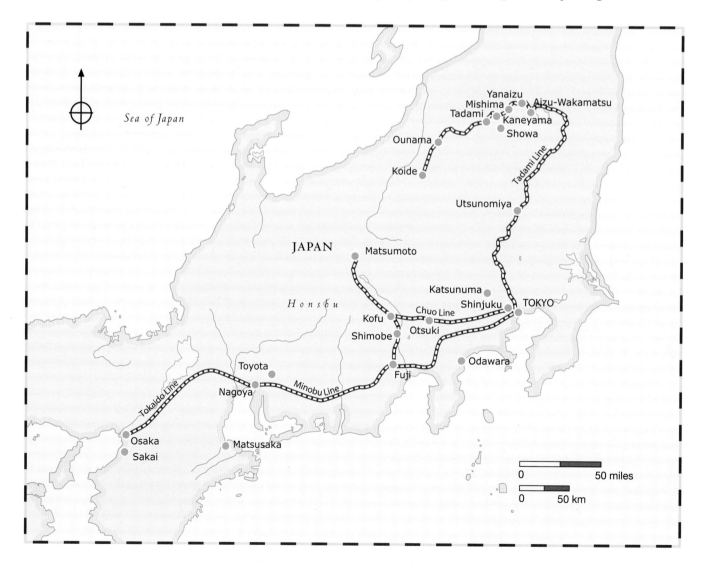

networks include winding single-track lines reaching way up into the nation's highest mountains.

Above One of Tokyo's busiest and most important train lines is the quadruple-track Yamanote Line operated by East Japan Railway Company (JR East)..

WELCOME ABOARD

Tokyo has numerous narrow-gauge routes, and among the busiest is the famous Yamanote Line, or 'Loop', which encircles the city centre, with numerous stations along the way. Among the stops are those at Akihabara, a busy area known for burgeoning discount electronic stores where discriminating shoppers can find the latest high-tech gadgetry. Others include the busy junction at Ueno near one of Tokyo's larger city parks and Shinjuku Station, which is claimed to be world's busiest railway station, with more than three million commuters passing through it on the average weekday. In addition to the Yamanote Loop, the route hosts a variety of other services over sections of the line. While the loop itself is largely double tracked, in places the route has six or more tracks running alongside each other.

The exceptionally busy traditional Tokaido Line connects Tokyo and Osaka. Heavy traffic on this route in the 1950s encouraged construction of the parallel *New Tokaido Shinkansen* (opened in 1964). Despite the pioneering high-speed line, the narrow-gauge line remains one of Japan's most heavily travelled lines.

Fuji, the city named after Japan's famous volcanic peak at 3,776 m (12,388 ft), is the junction for the wildly scenic Minobu Line that follows the Fuji River up into the mountains. The lower end of the line was opened in 1913, and by 1928 the route was completed to stretch over 88 km (55 miles), where it joins with the Chuo Line at Kofu. Today, both ends feature regional suburban services, while the central portion of the line has a less frequent service, primarily aimed at line-side mountain resort towns. Much of this route is just single main track, a relatively unusual operating condition in Japan.

Since 1956, in addition to all-stops local trains, the Minobu

Line has hosted a fancier service known as the *Fujikawa*. It took some time, but this train was eventually granted limited express status. Since 1987, when the old Japanese National Railways was reorganized into six regional privatized systems, this route has been part of the JR Central network, and in 1995 the *Shizouka–Fuji–Kofu Fujikawa Express* was re-equipped with specially decorated Class 373 EMUs (electric multiple units). These feature large windows and glass ends for a better view of the passing scenic landscape. The interior is decorated in pastel shades of lavender and burgundy, with white and grey accents that mimic the hues of blossoming cherry trees. One of the best times to ride the line is during April, when the cherry blossoms are in full bloom. There are numerous tunnels and tight curves on the line to add to the excitement.

The Chuo Line operated by JR East runs inland on a sinuous route from Tokyo to Kofu, before trending northwesterly to Matsumoto. This route hosts several finely appointed and named streamlined trains, including the distinctive *Super Azusa*. Since 1993, the service has used specially styled 12-car E351 trains that operate limited express runs over the length of the line. It travels from Shinjuku Station to Matsumoto Station in two hours and 35 minutes. Since 2001, a train called *The Kaiji*, mostly aimed at business clientele, has operated between Shinjuku and Kofu on an express 100-minute schedule. At Otsuki, the Fuji Kyuko Line diverges from the Chuo Line, with local services operating to scenic areas including views of Mount Fuji, which dominates the horizon from many parts of the region.

Kofu in Yamanashi Prefecture, located in a natural basin and surrounded by mountains, is an interesting stop on the Chuo Line. Nearby attractions include Yumura *onsen*, Kofu Castle and the picturesque Shosenkyo Gorge. Kofu is also the centre of Japan's wine industry, with Sadoya Winery located within walking distance of the railway station. Other wineries, such as Chateau Mercian and L'Orient, are situated in the nearby town of Katsunuma.

Among the fanciest but least known trains on the Japanese network are the overnight sleeping car trains between major cities. Although these have been in decline in recent years, several runs survive. The most upmarket is the *Tokyo-Ueno to Osaka Cassiopeia*, which has a 17-hour end-to-end schedule. Other runs include the evocatively named *Twilight Express* from Osaka to Sapporo on the island of Hokkaido.

Left The E001 Series *Train Suite Shikishima* has sleeping cars and is one of the world's most expensive and exclusive trains.

ATTENTION TO DETAIL

Various regional railway travel passes are available, in addition to the Japan Rail Pass. For example, the JR East Pass offers unlimited travel for five days on local and bullet trains. The Japan Rail Pass is available to non-Japanese travellers for seven, 14 or 21 consecutive days of travel and provides access to most trains, including bullet, limited express and local trains, and some bus services. These passes are slightly cheaper to purchase online outside of Japan than within the country. In addition, the various regions within the national network offer more localized passes, which are useful to those only travelling in specific parts of the country.

Right Chuo Line trains operate along a 53-km (33-mile) track between Tokyo and Takao.

Below The *Super Azusa* train operates between Shinjuku and Matsumoto Stations.

TADAMI LINE

The World's Most Romantic Railway

The Tadami Line on the JR East network has been labelled the most romantic railway in the world. This winding, mountainous railway connects Aizu-Wakamatsu in Fukushima with Koide Station in Niigata. While only covering 135 km (84 miles), a non-stop journey takes more than four hours due to the twists and turns. Travel north from Tokyo and alight at Koriyama Station for the JR Ban'etsu West Line to Aizu-Wakamatsu Station in the region of Oku-Aizu, where the Tadami Line starts. Passengers can admire a wealth of delights on the journey including the region's rivers, tunnels, mountains, lakes, villages, temples, a beech forest (a protected UNESCO Biosphere), *onsen* hot springs, flowers and the ever-changing scenery, depending on the season. This is a train line for all seasons, with a snow-covered landscape in winter and a kaleidoscope of vibrant hues in autumn. Alight at various stations to access the main towns and villages of Yanaizu, Mishima, Kaneyama, Showa and Tadami. One of the most popular stops is the Number One Tadami River Bridge Viewpoint outside the town of Mishima. Train enthusiasts will enjoy travelling on the KiHa110 and KiHa120 series carriages that operate on the line. The rail service recently celebrated 50 years of operation. Parts of the line were severed due to storm damage in 2011, and replacement bus services still operate on some sections. Visitor revenue is small because few venture to this part of Japan despite the dramatically beautiful landscape. This means that the costly but ongoing repairs to the line have been slow, although a full opening is planned.

HOKKAIDO'S LOCAL TRAINS

JAPANESE CONTRASTS

Hokkaido, the northernmost of Japan's four main islands, is now connected directly to the *Shinkansen* network. These high-speed bullet trains travel between Tokyo and Hakodate in the far south of the island, just across the Tsugaru Strait from the northern tip of Honshu Island. Just over a decade or so ago, this journey from Tokyo to Sapporo, the capital of Hokkaido, took more than a day and a half, including a ferry crossing. Trains now travel under the strait via the Seikan Tunnel, which commences on Honshu near the town of Aomori. The newer and faster trains operated by the East Japan Railway Company and known as the *Tohoku–Hokkaido Shinkansen* cover the distance in eight hours. *Shinkansen* trains operate to Hokodate in southern Hokkaido, where there is a change of train for Sapporo (bullet trains are expected to connect through to Sapporo by 2030).

Once in Hokkaido, it is the local trains that will be of greatest interest to those who love train exploration. Visitors can travel by local train to many destinations in every corner of Hokkaido, and most are accessible from Sapporo within a day's journey.

TRACK NOTES

Hokkaido has two of the world's fastest diesel-powered, narrow-gauge trains, the *Super Hokuto* and *Super Ozora* limited expresses, which operate on the Sapporo-Hakodate and Sapporo-Kushiro routes respectively, using tilting, multiple-unit train sets with top speeds of 130 km/h (80 mph). The average speeds of these trains are even more impressive when the often mountainous terrain, curving tracks and number of stops that each makes are taken into consideration.

The *Super Ozora* traverses the island's biggest mountain range, covering 348 km (217 miles) at an average speed of (88 km/h, 55 mph), which includes four intermediate stops. The *Super Hokuto* passes along the rugged Pacific Coast at an average speed of 91 km/h (57 mph) on its journey of 319 km (198 miles), which includes no fewer than 11 station stops. With this kind of performance and frequent service on both lines, these trains provide a very efficient mode of travel.

WELCOME ABOARD

For a unique Hokkaido rail experience, board one of several local

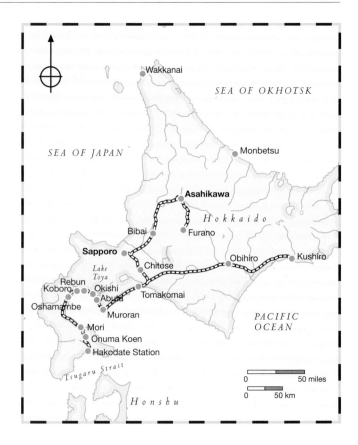

trains that operate on the island. Almost every stretch of railway on Japan's second largest island has a local passenger train that typically operates several services per day. The trains usually comprise one or two box-like, self-propelled diesel cars. They lack the sleek appearance and tilting mechanisms of the express trains, but most of them can still attain speeds of up to 115 km/h (70 mph), although few have the opportunity to hit top speed. Stations are spaced every few kilometres, even out in the countryside, and most local trains stop at every station along their respective routes. While travellers may spend longer on these trains, their time will not be wasted. Each local journey takes longer and provides a great opportunity to see more of the island and fully experience life on the train.

While the express trains whisk office workers from one meeting to another, the local trains cater to a more convivial clientele. Travellers who choose local trains have a greater opportunity to observe grandmothers on shopping trips and students going to and

Above A pair of KiHa 40 diesel multiple units climbs Jouman Pass on the Sekihoku Main Line in central Hokkaido.

from school. Except for kindergarten, there are no school buses in Japan, so older students regularly travel to school or college by train. You are likely to overhear groups of them practising English in hushed voices. If you are lucky, before they reach their stop the bravest in the group just might work up enough courage to strike up a conversation.

The same trip of 319 km (198 miles) from Sapporo to Hakodate, which takes three and a half hours by express, takes more than twice that by local train, and passengers have to change trains several times. Not all of the connections are tight, so there is time to explore some of the lesser known stops like Oshamambe. Leave the station, stroll the streets, find a noodle shop and ponder the changes that time has wrought on rural Hokkaido.

Hokkaido is the most recent major addition to Japan, fully colonized in the mid-1800s for its abundant natural resources. Its native people, the Ainu of Mongolian descent, were assimilated and few traces of Ainu culture remain. To learn more about them,

alight from the train at Shiraoi and take a short walk from the station. On the north side of the tracks, the Shiraoi Ainu Museum is arguably the finest museum about the Ainu people in all of Japan.

Coal, timber and seafood brought the Japanese to Hokkaido. Coal, in particular, led to rapid industrialization of the island. The journey between Sapporo and Hakodate traverses a section of one of the island's first railways, which connected several inland coal mines to the fabulous natural harbour of Muroran. To fully explore the harbour, leave the main line at Higashi-Muroran and take a journey of 6.5 km (4 miles) on the branch line along the Etomo Peninsula to Muroran proper. The ride passes steel mills operated by Nippon Steel Corporation.

Muroran's mills and Hokkaido's coal mines boomed through

the first two-thirds of the twentieth century, but then Japanese economic and energy policies changed. As cheaper coal began to be imported from China and Australia, Hokkaido's mines fell silent. Muroran's population plummeted from 160,000 in the 1960s to just 93,000 today. Mining towns in the interior, like Yubari, suffered far greater declines. Today, Hokkaido's capital of Sapporo is one of Japan's fastest growing cities, but on the whole the island's population is shrinking. With fewer jobs in the countryside, rural Hokkaidians are either moving to Sapporo or leaving the island altogether. The express trains travel so fast that you may not notice these changes, but if you ride the local trains you can spot the small detail everywhere.

South-west of Muroran, heading towards Hakodate, the scenery opens up and soon becomes quite dramatic. Abuta (Toya Station) is the gateway to Lake Toya, part of the Shikotsu-Toya National Park reached by a direct bus service from Toya Station. Beyond Abuta, the railway plays hide-and-seek with the bay, punching through a series of tunnels and clinging to a narrow, rocky shelf right beside the water. Winter sunsets can be fabulous in the late afternoons, while seaside camping is available in the warmer months near Rebun and Okishi Stations, which are only served by local trains.

To get about as far from civilization as you can go by train in Japan, disembark at Koboro Station, an unlikely stop right between two long tunnels. Originally built as a signal station, Koboro became an unofficial stop for local trains of the Japanese

National Railways. When Japan privatized its railways in 1987, Koboro was granted official station status. Some train experts rate it as the number one *hikyoh eki* (remote station) in the entire country. A trail leads down to a scenic, deserted beach in a small cove, while another trail leads to a larger cove that includes a Shinto shrine built into a cave. Those who are attracted to the prospects presented by this station should check carefully, as only half of the local trains stop at Koboro.

Further south, Onuma Koen Station provides access to Onuma Quasi National Park, which includes two lakes, miles of trails and the Mount Komagatake volcano. Hakodate is a charming seaport on Hokkaido's southern coast, with an extensive streetcar system, exquisite seafood and one of the best night views on the

Above A single KiHa 40 150 railcar passing rice fields along the Muroran Main Line near Abuta.

Opposite A local train stopping at the remote Koboro Station located between two long tunnels on the Muroran Main Line.

island. Mount Hakodate looks down on the heart of the city, built on the narrow isthmus between Hakodate Bay and the Tsugaru Strait. The strait connects the Pacific Ocean to the Sea of Japan and separates Hokkaido from Honshu, the largest island of the Japanese archipelago. Ferries still ply the strait, but since 1988 the Seikan Tunnel, measuring 54 km (33½ miles) in length, under the strait has connected Hokkaido to the rest of the Japanese railway network. Local trains do not operate through the tunnel, but

or literally 'Big Snow Mountains', are Hokkaido's backbone. Daisetsuzan National Park, the largest park in Japan, includes 16 peaks in excess of 2,000 m (6,560 ft), and extensive hiking and backpacking trails.

Those who venture to Kushiro might consider heading north up the Senmo Line through the wetlands of Kushiro-Shitsugen National Park, and on to Shiretoko National Park on the island's narrow northeastern peninsula.

Travel writer Paul Theroux explored Hokkaido and documented his journey in his 2008 book *Ghost Train to the Eastern Star*. His description of the train journey to and from Wakkanai is essential reading for those planning to ride the line all the way to Japan's northernmost railway station. The *Limited Express Super Soya 1* takes more than five hours to cover the distance. Wakkanai is a seaport where fishing trawlers head out into the Sea of Japan. It is also a popular destination for *onsen*, or soaking in the therapeutic waters of hot springs. In winter, the piping hot water in these baths contrasts markedly with the snow and sub-zero temperatures in the outdoors. There are other parts of the island, including Jozankei Hot Springs just south-west of Sapporo, where tourism is centred on thermal springs.

Car ferries operate to the two Japanese islands of Rishiri and Rebun off Wakkanai, and also to the Russian island of Sakhalin. These are weather dependent and can be unpredictable, especially during May and June.

ATTENTION TO DETAIL

The best times of year to take long trips by local trains are around the school holidays, when the *seishun juhachi kippu*, or youthful eighteen passes, are made available. Despite the name of the passes, travellers of any age can purchase them, and for a reasonable fee get five days of unlimited travel on local and rapid trains anywhere in the country (travelling days need not be consecutive). Travellers are still likely to share their rides with students, who will often be taking vacation trips of their own. There are three annual school holiday periods – March through early April, late July to early September, and early December to early January. With Hokkaido's mild summers, travellers can take advantage of another perk of local train travel during the warmer months – windows that actually open. Other passes can be used on Hokkaido, including the Japan Rail Pass and the Hokkaido Pass.

Below A KiHa 54 on Hokkaido's Senmo Line crossing the Shari River near the Shiretoko Peninsula.

Passengers who book tickets online will receive a QR code that can be exchanged for a hard-copy ticket at a self-service machine at any Japanese railway station. Tickets can also be purchased from the same machines, which accept coins and notes but not credit cards. International air travellers arriving in Hokkaido's New Chitose Airport can begin their island railway journeys of discovery as soon as they land, with New Chitose Railway Station being located beneath the terminal building.

Train travel on Hokkaido varies dramatically with the seasons, from snow-covered journeys in winter, to spring scenery of fields of blooming sunflowers and lavender.

Above A one-car local train bound for Furano climbs the Karikachi Pass on the Sekisho Line near Shintoku.

Wherever you go by local train in Hokkaido, or anywhere in Japan, you are sure to find adventure and a deeper understanding of the land and its people and of their connections to Japan's railways. The Japanese continue to grow up with trains, and especially their local trains. They ride them to school and to work, on business trips and for family vacations. Thanks in large part to the local trains, the railways of Japan are still a common thread in the fabric of everyday life.

SOUTH KOREA
SEOUL TO BUSAN

HIGH-SPEED KTX TRAIN

The state-owned Korean Railroad Corporation (KORAIL) operates in South Korea's two main cities, the capital Seoul and Busan (formerly Pusan) in the south. The fastest bullet train covers the distance of 417 km (259 miles) on what is known as the Gyeongbu Line in just over two hours, while the slowest KTX service takes three and a half hours. The slowest regular train takes almost six hours. These latter trains are known as ITX-Saemaeul and Mugunghwa, and while they are slower they take a more scenic route with fewer tunnels.

TRACK NOTES

It is possible to connect internationally to this train via ferry services from China and Japan. A ferry service between Vladivostok (for the Trans-Siberian Railway) has been suspended, so overland travellers from Europe need to travel on the *Trans-Mongolian Railway* and beyond via the Chinese ports of Tianjin or Qingdao for a ferry to South Korea and on to its rail network.

The initial KTX train technology was based on that used for France's high-speed train network. These trains were introduced in Korea in 2004 to operate at a top speed of 305 km/h (190 mph), although the rail infrastructure was designed for higher speeds. Subsequently, locally developed trains such as the HSR-350X and HUMU-430X were introduced, and both can operate at higher speeds.

Trains operate at Swiss-watch precision and are invariably always on time. Negotiating the system is relatively easy, as signs are in both English and Korean. Car numbers are usually marked on train platforms to ensure that passengers queue up for approaching trains at the appropriate locations. Main stations are well equipped with easily recognizable international dining concepts, and local treats on the entrance concourse and dine-in restaurants are usually located about the ground floor. On the train, passengers can place large-luggage items at dedicated storage area near carriage doors, or in racks above their seats. In-seat facilities include reclining backs, footrests, wi-fi and fold-down tables.

WELCOME ABOARD

The South Korean capital, Seoul, with almost 10 million residents, is a city on the move, with many traditional and contemporary attractions to admire before travelling south on the KTX. The principal tourist sites are palaces, including the largest, Gyeongbokgung (built in 1395), Lotte World Tower, one of the world's tallest buildings with 123 levels, Seoul Tower on Mount Namsan, the traditional village of Bukchon Hanok, Bongeunsa Buddhist Temple and Gwangjang Market. Korean cuisine, especially its street food and barbecues, is eagerly devoured by most visitors.

Despite KTX trains moving rapidly through the countryside, towns and cities, the scenery viewed through panoramic windows is picturesque, with rice fields, mountains, towns and cities. The double-track line terminates in Busan, a coastal port beside the Sea of Japan, and the Japanese island of Fukuoka just 100 km (60 miles) to the south-east. Being coastal, South Korea's second largest city is vastly different from Seoul with its beaches and a resort-like atmosphere.

Visitors to the country can use the train to visit national attractions along the route, including various sports venues used for the 1988 Seoul Summer Olympics. Alight from the train between Seoul and Osan for the Korean Folk Village – a living museum showcasing Korean homes and customs, plus dining options and a theme park. The Independence Hall of Korea, located near Cheonan-si, is a museum of Korean history and the nation's independence. The large indoor and outdoor market in Daegu is very popular with tourists who enjoy shopping while on their travels.

ATTENTION TO DETAIL

Bookings can be made on South Korean trains 12 months in advance, with the best online site to purchase tickets being the Letskorail website. An internet confirmation printout must be exchanged for a ticket at a station. Alternatively, purchase tickets at a station (ticket offices or machines), but try and avoid the busiest times of Friday and Sunday evenings plus holidays. A country-wide Korea Rail Pass (KR Pass) over a set number of days is also available to foreigners, but these passes cannot be used on metro or tourist-train services. Seating on the KTX is in first class (three seats across) or economy class (four seats across). First-class travellers enjoy complimentary snacks and some beverages inclusive of their ticket price.

Services commence at 5.15 a.m. from Seoul Station, with the last departing at 10.30 p.m., and trains make short scheduled stops at key stations along the way. There are 69 KTX departures each day. Ticket prices depend on the class of travel, day of the week and how far in advance the booking is made.

In 2016 a privately operated Super Rapid Train (SRT) began high-speed services from Seoul to Busan and Seoul to Mokpo (south-west coast). Trains to these two destinations depart from Seseo Station, on the outskirts of Seoul.

Below KTX high-speed bullet trains connect Korean cities just within a few hours on five different lines, with the most popular route connecting Seoul and Busan.

RESOURCES

USEFUL CONTACTS

Belmond www.belmond.com

Darjeeling Himalayan Railway www.in.net

Deccan Odyssey www.thedeccanodyssey.com

Eastern & Oriental Express www.orient-express.com

Indian Railways www.indianrail.gov.in

Indonesian Railways (P T Kereta Api) www.kai.id or www.tiket.com

Keretapi Tanah Melayu (KTM) www.ktmb.com.my

Korean Railways www.korail.com, www.letskorail.com

North Borneo Railway www.northborneorailway.com.my

Pakistan Railways www.pakrail.gov.pk

Palace on Wheels www.palaceonwheels.com

Royal Railways Cambodia www.royal-railway.com

Sabah State Railway www.railway.sabah.gov.my

Seven Stars in Kyushu www.cruisetrain-sevenstars.jp

Singapore MRT www.mot.gov.sg

Sri Lanka Railways www.railway.gov.lk

State Railway of Thailand www.railway.co.th

Taiwan Railway www.tip.railway.gov.tw

Viceroy Special www.jftours.com

Vietnam Railways www.vr.com.vn

FURTHER READING

Bowden, D. 2013. *Enchanting Bali*. John Beaufoy Publishing.

Bowden, D. 2014. *Enchanting Malaysia*. John Beaufoy Publishing.

Bowden, D. 2016. *Enchanting Borneo*. John Beaufoy Publishing.

Bowden, D. 2016. *Presenting Malaysia*. John Beaufoy Publishing.

Bowden, D. 2019. *Enchanting Indonesia*. John Beaufoy Publishing.

Bowden, D. 2019. *Enchanting Langkawi*. John Beaufoy Publishing.

Bowden, D. 2019. *Enchanting Penang*. John Beaufoy Publishing.

Bowden, D. 2019. *Enchanting Vietnam*. John Beaufoy Publishing.

Bowden, D. 2020. *Great Railway Journeys in Australia and New Zealand*. John Beaufoy Publishing.

Ellis, R. 1994. *Sri Lanka by Rail*. Bradt Publications.

Ellis, R. 1997. *India by Rail*. Bradt Publications.

Hilton, J. 1933. *Lost Horizons*. Macmillan.

Orwell, G. 1934. *Burmese Days*. Harper & Brothers.

Pallin, M. 2004. *Himalaya*. Weidenfeld and Nicholson.

Solomon, B. 2015. *The World's Most Exotic Railway Journeys*. John Beaufoy Publishing.

Solomon, B. 2020. *The World's Great Rail Journeys*. John Beaufoy Publishing.

Theroux, P. 1975. *The Great Railway Bazaar by Train through Asia*. Hamish Hamilton.

Theroux, P. 1988. *Riding the Iron Rooster by Train through China*. Hamish Hamilton.

Theroux, P. 2008. *Ghost Train to the Eastern Star*. Houghton Mifflin.

ACKNOWLEDGEMENTS

Many people contributed valuable insights and feedback in compiling this book. Particular thanks go to Elvira Arifullina (Russian Railways Press Service), Paul Bigland, Ole Bisbjerg, Russell Brown, Elizabeth Clarke (Windamere Hotel, Darjeeling), Juliet Coombe, Miguel Cunat, Shankar Dandapani (for travel on Indian trains), Chamindra Goonewardene (Resplendent Ceylon), Cassandra Graham, John Guiry and Chhayleak Kong (Royal Railways Cambodia), Noel Jayasekara (JF Tours and Travels), Hoàng Công Thành, Peter Jordan (Darjeeling Tours), Tania Joslin, Toby Law (Peak Tramways), Bertie Lawson (Sampan Travel, Myanmar), David Lim (EL SOL Travel & Tours, Malaysia), Scott Lothes, Karen Matsuyama (Kofu Tourism), Simon Metcalfe (Kyushu Tourist Promotion Organisation), David Michael (Sabah Tourism Board), Colin Nash, Yumiko Nishitani (Sakura PR), Pakistan Railway (Adeel Shahzad, Azhar Malik, Ijaz Malik, Shahbaz Hassan and Zahid Bhatti), Simon Pielow (Luxury Train Club), Andrew Philip Snow (Thailand-Burma Railway Centre), Sarantsetseg Khasbaatar (Mongolian Railway), Brian Solomon, Bernard Van Cuylenburg, Vinodh Wichremeratne, Bagus Widyanto (Indonesian Railway Tour) and Michael Zhou (Tang Dynasty Tours).

INDEX

First published in the United Kingdom in 2022 by John Beaufoy Publishing,
11 Blenheim Court, 316 Woodstock Road, Oxford OX2 7NS, England
www.johnbeaufoy.com

10 9 8 7 6 5 4 3 2 1

ISBN 978-1-913679-30-9

Designed by Ginny Zeal
Edited and indexed by Krystyna Mayer
Cartography by William Smuts
Project management by Rosemary Wilkinson

Printed and bound in Malaysia by Times Offset (M) Sdn. Bhd.